# POWER PLAYS
## FOR
# YOUTH GROUPS

# POWER PLAYS *for* YOUTH GROUPS

## Bill Hand

BAKER BOOK HOUSE
Grand Rapids, Michigan 49516

ISBN: 0-8010-4363-8

Scripture quotations are from the New International Version. Copyright © 1973, 1978, 1984 International Bible Society. Used by permission of Zondervan Bible Publishers.

Printed in the United States of America

**To**

the members of my drama group,
the *Hezekiah* Players
the longsuffering friends, guinea pigs,
Hitchcock's "Cattle"
Ron and Kim Fisher
Sari Fisher and Aaron Slater Fisher
Donna Baker
Bob and Linda Cook
Raymond Cook, Debbie Cook
Nancy and Allie Graff
Becky Burrows
Charlie Burrows
Julie Carnino
Karen Hand
(sister and *Hezekiah* member in spirit)

**and most important of all,**
**Roberta**
my wife
and come-on-you-can-do-it-er

# CONTENTS

*(For a listing of roles, male-female ratio, costume, set, and property requirements, see alphabetical index.)*

**Part One: A Few Fine Days in the Bible**

1. Brother's Keeper (Cain) | *Monologue*     13
   REBELLION, ANGER, COMMITMENT

2. A Real Stew (Esau) | *Comedy/Interview*     17
   PRIORITIES, COMMITMENT

3. Well-Pegged (Jael and Deborah) | *Comedy*     21
   WOMEN, RELATIONSHIPS

4. Advice and Adonijah (Adonijah) | *Monologue*     27
   REBELLION, PRAYER, SEEKING GOD'S WILL

5. A Matter of Worth (Elisha's servant) | *Comedy*     31
   GREED, OBEDIENCE

6. The Puppet Master (Judas' decision to betray) | *Poetic Drama*     37
   TEMPTATION, ANGER, REBELLION, SATAN

**Part Two: The Daniel Skits**

*(These skits may be performed either as a full presentation in six scenes, or as individual skits. The theme of the series is peer pressure.)*

Intro     45

7. The Friends Who Obeyed God (Chapter 1) | *Skit*     47
   OBEDIENCE, PEER PRESSURE, COMMITMENT

8. The King's Dream (Chapter 2) | *Skit*     51
   WISDOM, OBEDIENCE, PROPHECY

9. The Fiery Furnace (Chapter 3) | *Skit*     55
   PRAYER, OBEDIENCE, TRUST, GOD'S PROTECTION

10. The Dream of the Tree (Chapter 4) | *Skit*     59
    PRIDE

11. The Handwriting on the Wall (Chapter 5) | *Skit*     65
    PRIDE, IMMORALITY, JUDGMENT

12. The Lions' Den (Chapter 6) | *Skit*     69
    PRAYER, OBEDIENCE, TRUST, GOD'S PROTECTION, COMMITMENT

**Part Three: Taking on the World**

13. The Fable of the New Age Pig | *Comedy/Fable*     75
NEW AGE

14. The Procedure | *Drama*     81
EUTHANASIA

15. Not Just Black and White | *Drama*     85
ABORTION

**Part Four: All About God and Christians**

16. Judgment Jeopardy | *Comedy/Game Show*     93
JUDGMENT, COMMITMENT, SALVATION, CONSISTENT LIVING

17. Restaurant Christians | *Comedy*     99
CONSISTENT LIVING, PRAYER

18. The Education Interview | *Comedy/Interview*     105
CONSISTENT LIVING

19. Manna Helper | *Commercial Spoof*     109
CONSISTENT LIVING, THANKFULNESS

20. The Quicker Moral-Upper | *Commercial Spoof*     111
CONCERN, PAT ANSWERS

21. Spiritually Fed | *Comedy*     113
CONSISTENT LIVING, CHURCH LIFE

22. What's the Answer? | *Comedy/Drama*     121
LOVE, SALVATION, MISSIONS

23. The Reunion | *Comedy/Drama*     127
PRAYER, WITNESS, MISSIONS

24. Ice Men | *Historical Drama*     133
WITNESS, COMMITMENT, SUFFERING

25. Second Habakkuk | *Poetic Drama*     137
CONCERN, PRAYER, MISSIONS

26. The Savage | *One-Act Drama*     141
CONCERN, JUDGMENTALISM, MISSIONS

Appendix: Directing Holy Thespians     151

Alphabetical Index of Plays     165

# A NOTE FROM THE PLAYWRIGHT

Few teaching tools are more powerful than humor and drama. An illustration acted out can clarify, challenge, and provoke in ways that wordy sermons never can. In its earliest form among the Greeks drama was a teaching tool. For centuries the church has taught man's redemption and God's love through drama—and humor was usually an important element.

The skits in this collection point out biblical truths through allegory and familiar Bible stories, primarily by means of sharp, thought-provoking humor (although you'll find a few serious skits as well).

Varied and contemporary, these programs meet almost any need. The styles range from gentle to outright slapstick, and the roles require from one to twenty actors. The skits include challenging roles for talented thespians as well as traditional, wordless walk-ons for those who are shy or awkward at public speaking.

The sets are primarily simple—a few chairs or nothing at all, with possibly a painted backdrop made of cardboard. One or two skits call for more elaborate settings, but none are too difficult for your congregation's favorite handyman.

Performance times range from one minute to twenty.

Each skit also includes a brief meditation and Scripture references for use as an opener to readings, rehearsals, and programs.

Use these for Youth Sunday or youth rallies; as a street ministry; as a witnessing program to juvenile rehabilitation centers, handicapped centers, and nursing homes; or as programs for other churches. You might make a video of some of these skits for a fund-raiser. A couple (see *Restaurant Christians* and *The Quicker Moral-Upper*) might even work as a challenging, impromptu skit at a local eatery.

Make these skits special. Challenge your actors to memorize their parts—they're up to it; I guarantee it. Direct them with flair and encourage your actors to do their best! If you've never or rarely directed before, don't panic. I've included a minicourse titled "Directing Holy Thespians" in the appendix.

Also at the back you will find a helpful, alphabetically arranged index listing each play and its requirements regarding actors, sets, costumes, and props.

For a more thorough lesson on directing and acting, I am available for weekend seminars. Write me for information at this address:

Bill Hand
125 Furnace Road
Greenville, PA 16125

Feel free to write and let me know if there are any topics or areas you'd like to see that weren't covered here. I'd also love to hear how this collection has been used to bless and benefit your youth.

Godspeed on your efforts to be genuine fools for Christ!

Bill Hand
Spring, 1991

# PART ONE

## A Few Fine Days
## in the Bible

# 1

# BROTHER'S KEEPER

"If you do what is right, will you not be accepted? But if you do not do what is right, sin is crouching at your door" (Gen. 4:7a).

You know Cain, subject of the oldest joke known to man ("He killed his brother because he was Abel"). His was not an unusual crime, in history or in the Bible. Many killed—or at least tried to kill—their brothers. Look at Joseph's. Abimelech, son of Gideon, killed sixty-nine of his seventy brothers (Judg. 9:5). Absalom killed Amnon for making improper advances toward his sister, Tamar (2 Sam. 13).

Cain's whole story is crowded into a very short passage—Genesis 4:1–16. Still, his is the most famous murder in the history of man. Why? In part, because his was the *first* murder—the first major fruit of his parents' sin. Secondly, because of the motive. Abimelech killed for power. Absalom killed for revenge. Other brothers throughout history have killed in fits of passion. Cain killed out of jealousy over God's favor. His was an ultimate act of rebellion against God.

Equally outstanding was his total lack of repentance: when God called him on his act, he felt worse about his punishment than his crime. More than anyone else in the Bible, Cain represents the fallen man in full-blown rebellion, still loved and protected by God, pressing God toward ultimate judgment.

\* \* \*

*Character:*
    CAIN

*Props:*

(At start): a loaf of unsliced bread and a large, sharp knife on a breadboard; a jar of peanut butter with a table knife.

Scene two: a grocery bag. In it: an apple, cans of asparagus (Green Giant brand), mandarin oranges, pineapple chunks, Pepperidge Farm soup, and possibly other canned goods.

*Set:* A kitchen table, a couple of chairs.

## SCENE ONE

*Cain enters, his hair mussed, his eyes always hostile and angry. He takes a large knife and cuts a slice of bread from a loaf. He makes a peanut butter sandwich as he talks, sometimes to himself, sometimes to the audience.*

CAIN    Abel—thinks he is such a hotshot! He comes over to see what I'm gettin' ready to give in the offering . . . so I take him to my room and I show him a couple piles of veggies I grew. "Hey, that's a nice tomato," he says. "That'll make a radical offering." I say, "You dweeb . . . that's for 4-H. Here's the pile I'm usin' for the offering." So he strolls over, picks up a tomato, and says, "Little soft spot here."

I say, "Oh, really?"

He says, "Oh, yeah, right here. Look, it's all gray-blue. Want me to getcha another one?"

"Naw. If I want another tomato with a soft spot, I'll just drop one on the floor."

He just looks at me. Then he says, "I'll getcha a better one."

"What for?"

"You don't want to give God bad stuff."

"I'm gonna burn it, not feed it to 'im."

He gets this horrified look on his face. "You give God your best stuff. He'll know if you don't."

I say, "Look, you fill the requirements, that's all that matters. So what are *you* givin' him?"

"One of my sheep." What else is he gonna give him? He's a shepherd!

"Which one, Einstein?"

"That little one that was born last week."

"The spotted one, huh? The one with the gimp?"

"No. The best one, all white. The firstborn."

I hate that uppity little dweeb.

*He starts to go, then stops.*

I have this theory: little brothers are a result of the fall.

*He exits.*

## SCENE TWO

*Table as before, with loaf of bread, knife, peanut butter. Cain enters, carrying a bag of groceries, which he sets down on the table. He begins removing items, starting with an apple from which he takes an occasional bite.*

CAIN   I been thinkin' about Abel, and I know what he's up to. He's tryin' to show me up . . . figures his sheep are better'n my veggies. Figures he can get God to love him more than he loves me. Competition, man. It always comes down to competition.

But I got 'im. An' I didn't have to bust my back in the garden all day to do it . . . I went to the source and got the best! *[He pulls a can out of the bag.]* Green Giant! Lookit this stuff . . . asparagus. You know how long it takes to grow good asparagus? Some guy broke his back over that. It cost *me*, too—a buck and a half, even on sale! God'll notice that, I'll bet. And look here: mandarin oranges. Pineapple chunks in their juices, man . . . none of that sugar stuff. Hey, get this: Pepperidge Farm soup. Not generic. Not even Campbell's chunky. This is Pepperidge Farm. Quality stuff.

I blew a wad on all this stuff. God's gonna forget Abel ever existed. *[He examines a can and flips it in the air, catching it again.]* I got more in the truck. Soon as someone invents a can opener, I'm in business.

*He exits.*

## SCENE THREE

*Table as before: bread, knife, peanut butter, canned goods. Cain enters in a fury.*

CAIN   **I DON'T BELIEVE IT!**

*He kicks over a chair and roars.*

CAIN  **HE DIDN'T TAKE IT!**

*He throws himself onto the other chair and, roaring, bangs his head on the table three times. Then he pounds the table with his fists three times . . . then he pounds the table with his fists and his head several times, roaring guttural sounds all the while. He looks up at the audience.*

CAIN  It isn't fair! First, no one invents a can opener, so I'm sittin' out there, all day long, beating cans with a rock! *[Now he begins angrily making a peanut butter sandwich.]* I smashed my fingers! My blisters' blisters have blisters! Nobody tells me all this stuff is packed in water, so when I empty the cans on the altar, the fire goes out! All day long I fan the fire, all it does is smoulder! Abel waltzes up with his lamb, cuts its throat, burns it up—twenty minutes flat. Then the prayer: I've worked on this prayer for days . . . try it out on everyone in the world, almost—Mom and Dad! I deliver it without a flaw . . . all Abel does is whip some praisey stuff off the top of his head. I outdid that dweeb right down the line! And whose offering gets accepted?

*He slams the knife into the bread.*

CAIN  ABEL'S! I go into a fury. Mom is cryin', Dad's flippin' out, and Abel's yellin' it's okay. Sure, it's okay! God *took* his offering!

I take off to my private place, down in the thorns. Everybody's lookin' for me. Of course, God finds me. He's worse than a parent.

"Cain, why're you angry? Why're you so downcast? If you do what's right, won't I accept you? But if you don't do what's right, sin is crouching at your door; it desires to have you, but you must master it." Sounds like Shakespeare.

Apparently my sacrifice isn't right. What, Abel's is? "His heart's in the right place!" Where's mine, in my armpit? How'm I gonna be number one with God with that kind of competition around? What'm I gonna do?

*END*

# 2

# A REAL STEW

"So Esau despised his birthright" (Gen. 25:34b).

Esau is the original "dumb jock." I can't help but feel a little sorry for him. After all—his brother Jacob was no sweetheart. Always scheming to set himself up—first for a birthright, then an inheritance, then the best part of Laban's sheep. He even tried to scheme for God's blessing, until God outschemed *him*. If I were to portray Jacob and Esau as contemporary men, I'd cast Esau as a tackle for the 49ers and Jacob as the head of a national chain of used car dealerships.

Why did God allow the schemer to get the blessing over his brother who, after all, was duped right out of his pants? I guess it can best be explained like this: Jacob was full of human weaknesses, not the least of which were greed and selfishness. But through the years God was able to deal with these attitudes (and Jacob's seeds produced some very bitter crops—read his story to see how often his crimes came back to camp at his front door). Jacob's faith overrode his baser traits. He loved God.

And—*bingo*—Esau didn't. The big oaf wasn't just surrendering the better portion of a bunch of sheep and leadership of a clan—he was selling off God's promises for a bowl of soup! To have been so easily bilked, he must have had little regard for the Lord and his blessings. As the writer of Genesis pointed out, Esau didn't just have little concern for his birthright—he *despised* it.

\* \* \*

*Characters:*
> Dan Ratter, Correspondent
> (or, if played by a female,
> Murky Brown)
>
> Rebekah, Jacob's mother
> Jacob
> Esau

*For a list of props, see index, page 167.*

RATTER    This is the evening news. I'm Dan Ratter. Trouble: it's all in the family for world-renowned patriarch Isaac. In an unprecedented move, Esau has sold his birthright to his brother Jacob for an unnamed sum. We now bring you this exclusive interview.

*Enter Rebekah.*

RATTER    With us now is Rebekah, Isaac's beloved wife and the mother of Jacob and Esau. They're twins, right?

REBEKAH    That's right. Born together, they were, all tangled up and that's how they've been ever since. Good boys, both of them, but especially Jacob.

RATTER    Would you say you have a favorite?

REBEKAH    A mother never has a favorite. They're both equal in my eyes.

RATTER    I see.

REBEKAH    Jacob being the most equal of the two.

RATTER    Pardon?

REBEKAH    Esau can be such an oaf. Big, hairy, bright as corrugated cardboard. You know?

RATTER    No, I don't.

REBEKAH    Hunt and hunt, hunt and hunt. Only thing he knows. Every day he hauls in something else and dumps it at my feet. He says, "Look, Ma!" I say, "Very nice, son. What is it?" He says, "It's an ostrich, Ma!" I say, "Very nice, son. What am I supposed to do with it?" He says, "Clean it, Ma!" I just get that bird plucked and cleaned when in he comes with something else. "Look, Ma!" "Nice, son. What's this one?" "Groundhog, Ma!" "How nice, son." "Clean it, Ma!" Ten minutes later he drags in a buck, then a lion, then a yak. He's worse than the cat. I send him out to check up on the flock. Next thing I know, I'm neck-deep in dead sheep. "Clean 'em for me, Ma!" I've seen enough innards in a day to wrap three times around Palestine, you know?

RATTER    I . . . uh . . . see.

REBEKAH    Long and pink and smelly.

RATTER    [Getting ill] Yes, but . . .

REBEKAH    Furs, I can sell. Feathers, I can sell. But what am I supposed to do with all those innards?

RATTER    Well . . . ulp . . .

REBEKAH    I tried stringing tennis rackets.

RATTER    Tennis rackets?

REBEKAH    Nice heirlooms. You never know when one of your descendants will be serving in somebody's courts. The things sure do get rank in the sun, though.

RATTER    Urp . . .

REBEKAH    But that Jacob, what a nice boy. Just like his Mom. Delicate features, quick mind, treats me good. Just hangs around the fire all day and helps with the cooking. Alan Alda before his time, you know? You never see him dropping dead animals at my feet. He's got a good head on his shoulders, but his father doesn't see it. Just makes me shudder to think of Esau getting the birthright and being the next patriarch, you know? I can just see it now. "Here, Ma! It's an elephant for the sacrifice! Can ya clean it?"

*Enter Jacob.*

RATTER    Ah, here is Jacob, himself.

JACOB    Hey, Dan. How's the cardigan sweater I sold you?

RATTER    I've been meaning to talk to you about that. When I took it out of the box, it didn't have any sleeves.

JACOB    Hey, I told you it was twenty percent off.

RATTER    We were just discussing Esau's birthright.

JACOB    Oh, yeah. Esau. Nice kid, but a little slow.

RATTER    Yes, but . . .

18

JACOB   Still, he's got his good points. You should see him standing sideways in a breeze. He sticks a finger in one ear and, depending on how he turns it, he can make the wind play "Dixie" when it whistles through.

RATTER   But what about his birthright?

JACOB   *My* birthright.

REBEKAH   *Your* birthright?

JACOB   He sold it to me last night. I was going to tell you.

RATTER   How did you get him to sell you something as important as his birthright?

JACOB   He just doesn't think ahead. And he doesn't respect the value of things. He's out hunting all day, see, and I knew he'd be hungry when he got back. So I fixed up his favorite: red stew.

RATTER   What is red stew?

JACOB   Potatoes, lightly boiled. With innards.

RATTER   I had to ask.

JACOB   So in comes Esau and he starts sniffing the air and smacking his lips. "Is that what I think it is?" he asks. I say, "It's red stew." He says, "I'm hungry. Give me a bowl." I give him a bowl and he says, "I meant a bowl with red stew in it." I tell him, "The bowl's free. The stew'll cost you." He says, "How much?" I say, "Your birthright."

RATTER   And he said yes? He sold his birthright, his inheritance, for a bowl of stew?

JACOB   He says, "I'm so hungry I'll die if I don't eat. What good's my birthright if I'm dead?" So he made the deal.

RATTER   Don't you feel bad about tricking him like that?

JACOB   Hey, he's only older by a minute. Besides, a guy who's willing to sell off his entire birthright for soup deserves to lose it.

REBEKAH   You know, a birthright isn't much good without your father's blessing to go with it. He'll never give it willingly, but I've got this great idea about how we can trick him into it. You know how blind that man's become. . . .

RATTER   Aren't you worried that God will make you pay for fooling Esau and Isaac like that?

REBEKAH   *[Ignoring him]* Here's what you do. First, the next time Esau's out hunting, you fix your father a pot of stew. Then, get some goat skin and tie it to your arms, so you'll be all hairy and smelly like Esau.

*They exit as Esau enters. He carries a bowl, the contents of which he is finishing off with his fingers. He then licks his fingers clean.*

RATTER   Esau, how could you have sold your birthright for a bowl of stew?

ESAU   It's good stew.

RATTER   But to get it, you gave up your right to your father's inheritance, your right to carry on his name!

ESAU   Don't knock it till you've tasted this stew.

RATTER   But think! Was it worth it?

ESAU   Look, if a guy don't eat, he dies. Then what good's an inheritance?

19

RATTER    You weren't going to die if you didn't get that stew! All you had to do was wait until supper.

ESAU    Supper?

RATTER    You know, the evening meal.

ESAU    *[As if this had never occurred to him]* Oh, yeah. Supper.

RATTER    You didn't use your head; you didn't think about the consequences of your actions! As a result, you've been bilked of your inheritance by your little brother!

ESAU    My little brother did that?

RATTER    Of course, you let him.

ESAU    My sweet little brother?

RATTER    And now, God's promise will be carried on through Jacob, because you despised that promise for the sake of soup!

ESAU    My dead sweet little brother. *[He starts off]* Still, it *was* good stew. I think I'll do some hunting while I think about this. *[He tosses a dead animal—a teddy bear or something—at Ratter.]* Clean this, will ya?

RATTER    A simple act, a stupid act. Jacob was deceitful, and we can be sure he'll pay a price for that. But Esau put no value on God's promise or his own future, and we can be sure that history will remember him for being a man who put himself in a real stew. I'm Dan Ratter. Good night.

*END*

# 3

# WELL-PEGGED

"Because of the way you are going about this, the honor will not be yours, for the LORD will hand Sisera over to a woman" (Judg. 4:9b).

I am thinking back to my days at a conservative Christian college. One Bible professor had spent most of a semester pounding into us his belief that the Bible proved that women must be submissive and that, indeed, women are such second-class creations that they should hold no position of leadership in the church. One student sheepishly raised her hand and asked, "What about Deborah?"

Ah, yes, what *about* Deborah? And what about her somewhat unusual contemporary, Jael, who had the strange honor of driving a tent peg through the head of Israel's chief enemy? (Judg. 4:4–22).

The great theologian Paul insisted that man is to be the head of his household and the church, but being head does not imply being master—especially not an egotistical one. In today's church—and this has been true through modern history—men often refuse to come through on the leadership roles they so proudly claim. So, what is a woman to do? Watch her house and church collapse for fear of invading a man's castle? We can be thankful for Deborah, a woman in a man's world who was willing to take the reins when men failed God; and the nation of Israel had to be grateful for Jael, for without her bold action, the Israelites would certainly have had to face Sisera again.

* * *

*Characters:*
  NARRATOR
  BARAK, a Hebrew general
  DEBORAH, a Hebrew prophetess
  SISERA, a General of Hazor
  JAEL

*For list of props, see index, page 167.*

*The following skit is done in two vignettes.*

## SCENE ONE

*Deborah's Tree*

NAR   In the days of the judges, the evil general Sisera oppressed the Israelites for twenty years. But when they cried out, God raised up Deborah to be their judge, and Barak was the brave general, ready to face all odds.

*Deborah sits at her tree. She is passionate, like Joan of Arc. Barak comes running frantically, terrified.*

BARAK   Deborah!

DEB   I am here, Barak.

BARAK   Sisera is down there!

21

DEB   I know.

BARAK   He's got nine hundred chariots!

DEB   I know.

BARAK   How are we ever going to defeat him?

DEB   *I know.*

BARAK   You do? How?

DEB   *[Looking at him]* The answer is right before me!

BARAK   It is? *[He spins and looks around. No one is there.]* Where?

DEB   *[Mysteriously]* God says, "I will lure Sisera to the Kishon River and give them into your hands!"

BARAK   Whose hands?

DEB   The man who stands right here with us.

*Again he looks around. There is nobody. Her meaning begins to dawn on him.*

BARAK   But . . . uh . . . there's only the two of us.

DEB   Take it a step further, professor.

BARAK   Only one of us is a man.

DEB   And which of us is the man? You? Or me?

BARAK   *[Swallows hard]* He's got . . . nine hundred chariots.

DEB   Don't you trust God?

BARAK   Of course! I shall lead Israel against this dog Sisera!

DEB   Of course!

BARAK   He will succumb to the mighty power of God!

DEB   *[More excited]* Of course!

BARAK   *[Raising his sword]* We will show him the result of fooling with God's people!

DEB   *[More excited yet]* But of course!

BARAK   And only one thing remains to be done before I go! And that is . . . *[Suddenly he begins to cry, blubbering for a moment before saying:]* Talking you into going with me!

*He runs, wailing, and throws himself at Deborah's feet. She shrugs her shoulders and throws up her hands in disgust.*

DEB   Of course! Be a man!

BARAK   Only if you'll be one with me!

DEB   You're making a fool of yourself!

BARAK   It's better than making a corpse of myself! You have to go! You're braver! You're strong! The men believe in you! *I* believe in you! I need you!

DEB   All right! All right! I'll go! But . . . ! God says because of how you are going about this the honor of taking Sisera himself will not be yours. Instead, Sisera will fall into the hands of a woman.

BARAK   Whatever you say, Deborah.

22

DEB   *[Rising]* Now come! You've a war to win for God and his children!

*She exits, dragging him along by the ear.*

## SCENE TWO

*Jael's Tent*

NAR   As the Lord predicted, Barak, with Deborah in tow, won a mighty battle that day: not a man of Sisera's army escaped. Sisera, however, fled on foot to the tent of Jael, the wife of Heber. You see, there were friendly relations between Sisera's king and Heber's clan.

*The scene is now the tent of Jael. Jael comes out of the tent carrying a mallet and a tent peg.*

JAEL   God! I've got you so well-pegged! You hate women, don't you! Look at what you've created! The men run the house! The men run the country! The men get to hunt and fish while we women have to clean the smelly hides and mend the tents and do the cooking! You're just like that worthless Heber says! We never get an honor! We never get the fun! You've set up creation so that we are only slaves to the whims of beasts! You give us labor pains! You even make us live longer than men so that we can enjoy our suffering that much longer! You give us . . . !

*She stops and glances at the ground.*

JAEL   A bug! *[Looking up]* Excuse me.

*She sneaks forward, raises her mallet, aims her tent peg and—WHAM! she nails the little sucker.*

JAEL   *[To audience]* Got 'im! *[Picking him up]* Disgusting little bug. Disgusting little, crawly little, black-hearted little, MALE bug!

*[Again she wails to the Almighty]* Oh, God, how tough it is to be a woman! If only you would show me that I'm worth as much in your sight as a man! If only a woman could be the deliverer of Israel for once! If only a man could be put at my mercy for once! If only you would decree that, SOMEtimes, a woman is better than a man! *[She sits and sighs.]*

*Sisera enters. He is a man who has lost a great battle: terrified, panting, out of breath, his eyes blackened, wearing torn clothes. He is a real mess.*

SISERA   Save me!

*Jael looks up to see Sisera, quickly hides her tent peg and mallet beneath her robe, then scrambles to her feet.*

JAEL   Who are you?

SISERA   *[Coming to her, trembling]* Sisera! I'm the general of King Jabin. He's a friend of your husband, Heber.

*She wanders around him, amused, looking him over carefully, studying his costume.*

JAEL   Is it Halloween already?

SISERA   I was in a battle with Barak the Israelite.

JAEL   *[Playing dumb]* Oh? How'd it go? *[As he answers, she stands there, examining her nails.]*

SISERA   *[Growing more panicked as he speaks]* Terrible! Just terrible! He clashed! We clashed! Our clothes clashed! Fighting! Swords! Spears! Chariots bogged down! Mayhem! Blood! Terror! Death! Defeat! *[Suddenly he calms down and says, matter of factly,]* Of course, you wouldn't understand; you're a woman.

*She looks at him sharply, without turning her head.*

SISERA    *[Now panicked again]* I've been running all day. I can't run any longer. Wait! You can help!

JAEL    *[Mock-innocent]* Realllly? You think so?

SISERA    Yes! Barak thinks you're on his side. You can hide me! In your tent! Just for a day or so! Then I can go back to the king. Yes! You can do it! You *must* do it!

JAEL    *[Childlike]* I dunno if I wanna.

*At first, Sisera reacts with horror—then he asserts himself.*

SISERA    Woman! Who said you had a choice?

JAEL    *[Distractedly]* Well, I did. Heber's not home, and that kind of makes me man of the tent, you might say, and . . .

SISERA    You WILL help me! You will hide me! It is my *will* that you hide me and it would be the will of your husband! What do you say to that?

JAEL    *[At the top of her lungs]* BAAAARAAAA-AAAK!

*In terror Sisera slaps his hand over her mouth to shut her up, cutting her off in mid-shout. He starts to release the grip, and the long call of Barak's name continues. He covers her mouth again.*

SISERA    *[Very humble]* I'll let you go. You do what you want.

*She nods. He lets go. He falls at her feet, clinging to her legs.*

SISERA    *Please* save me! Hide me! Help me! PLEASE!

JAEL    *[Like a schoolgirl]* Well, since you put it that way, how can I refuse? Besides, you're kinda cute, ya know? I don't know about all this bloody stuff and such, but I think I know just what I can do for ya. You just trust ol' Jael, and she'll do you just right.

SISERA    *[Sitting]* Oh, yes!

JAEL    *[Stepping behind him and massaging his shoulders]* You need some nice rest.

SISERA    That's right.

JAEL    Some warm milk!

SISERA    You're just like my momma.

JAEL    *[Viciously, as she gets him the glass of milk]* Not quite!

SISERA    What?

JAEL    *[Sweetly, as if speaking of the massage]* This right?

SISERA    Perfect! Oooh! My temples are throbbing.

*Jael begins to rub his temples. As Sisera continues to talk, she pulls a small target from her cloak and quietly pins it to his hair, so that it hangs over his temple.*

SISERA    My defeat wasn't the end of the world. A couple of days here, a little rest . . .

JAEL    You'll get plenty of rest.

SISERA    I'll go home, rebuild my army. We'll come back in a couple of years and Barak will be history. It's so nice of you to help me like this. I think I'll go and lie down now.

*He stands up and Jael steps back. Sisera exits to the tent and, before ducking in, says,*

SISERA    We'll get these Hebrews yet. You've been a wonderful handmaid to me. That's the wonderful thing about you women. You know how to serve your men. You knew my needs. You have me so well-pegged!

JAEL    *[Waving him off]* Oh, not really!

*He ducks into the tent. She pulls out her tent peg and mallet.*

JAEL    But I will pretty soon! *[She looks to God and grins.]* What I said earlier, God? I take it back!

*END*

# 4

# ADVICE AND ADONIJAH

"But in fact God has arranged the parts in the body, every one of them, just as he wanted them to be. If they were all one part, where would the body be?" (1 Cor. 12:18–19).

"Now Adonijah put himself forward and said, '*I* will be king'" (from 1 Kings 1:5). He wasn't concerned as to how he could best help the kingdom. He didn't bother to pray about his future and learn the will of God in this nation of God. He simply decided, "Hey—*I* wanna be king."

Everyone wants to be top dog, and very few people are happy with being servants. If they can't receive personal glory for a job, they don't want to do it. It's *beneath* them. But what good's an army with no soldiers? How can a government run if everyone is President and none are willing to be aides?

Read 1 Corinthians 12 and see: every part of the body is vital, each role as important as every other. As a body we uphold and benefit one another. As a massive collection of eyes we're nothing more than material for a Stephen King novel.

The story of Adonijah trying so desperately to make himself king, even though a better choice—God's choice—is available and known, is the story of many Christians in the body today.

* * *

*Character:*
UNCLE FESTUS (or maybe AUNT MARTHA)

*Uncle Festus comes out, an old-timer (or maybe it's Aunt Martha?) with a slow, drawling voice and an immensely easygoing manner. He begins by looking over the audience and focusing on a particular younger person as he begins his speech.*

"Now, onc't again you have come to me a-seekin' advice, tellin' me you have stumbled, as it were, upon a in-credible opportunity in your young life, an' that, if you move quick, you can seize it before someone else does. You say you want my opinion on the matter, an' you want it now, and I will jus' tell you this, an' this alone: go ask th' Almighty an' if it's okay with him, well, it's okay with me.

*He begins to leave, thinks better of it, and returns.*

"I don't know what the good Lord has in mind for you, but I do know this: if everyone who wanted to be chief was to become such, we would be right out of Indians, and the sitee-ation would be jus' like Congress.

*Satisfied, he turns to go, thinks better of it, and returns.*

"As a follerer of the good Lord Almighty, you of course want his will in your life and of course you want him to make you the top bug on the hill, but it may very well be he prefers you as a bug in the cellar, for them bugs is vital too.

"Now a bug in the cellar ain't no less important than the bug what's on the hilltop, at least not in the good Lord's sight. And besides, the bug what's on the hilltop didn't start up there. He started at the bottom, where he proved to the good Lord he could *handle* the hilltop—assumin', of course, a bug really cares whether he's in the cellar or on a hilltop, or even knows the differ'nce. It don't make no mind, anyhow. I jus' bring it up as a illustration, you understand.

*Okay. The point is made. He goes. But stops. And returns. Now he sits and really winds into his tale.*

"All this reminds me of a feller named Adonijer—maybe you don't recall him, but he was a son of old King David, and *I* recall him well enough. Not that I am so old as to have known the boy, mind you. But I read of him in the First Book of Kings, Old Testyment, an' what I read was enough that I wouldn't want him as no friend, anyhow.

"Now, King David was gettin' on in years, an' sometimes his head wasn't just right. He was forgetful, and irritable, and cold all the time. That is the way with some folks. Now David and his wife Bathsheeber had a intellygent young son named Solomon, and God had told them early on that this boy would be the next king.

"'Course, Adonijer would have none of that. He would not be a bug in the cellar, if you recall our little illustration, an' if you don't I don't blame you.

"No, he would be king. He did not see his father's side of the matter, an' did not care fer Bathsheeber's side, since she was not his mama at all—David had more wives than Brigham Young, you understand. He did not know God's side on the matter, neither, fer he did not bother to check.

"He was a bright boy, in the underhanded ways that boys will be bright, so he talked to some bigwigs who he knew might help make his kingship agreeable. He talked to Joab, who was a little

miffed with the king fer reasons we will not bother with now, so of course Joab was happy at the thought of pullin' one over on David. Then he talked to David's priest Abiathar, who was a man of some repute. He was happy with these fellers, fer he knew the kingdom would think of David whenever they'd come about, an' so they'd think of David when they saw him, as well.

"To close the whole deal, he rousted up fifty of David's chariots and messengers whom he would use to declare himself king throughout the land. David did nothing to stop this—you will recall I told you his head was not always just right these days—so Adonijer begun to figger he had his father's blessin' as well. Off he went to a nearby town fer a feast an' a coronation, an' he invited all the important people t' come an' see.

"'Course, he didn't realize God wanted someone else as top bug. But I won't bring that illustration up agin, fer it didn't work, somehow.

"Now, Nathan, who was a prophet of David, found out about Adonijer's little scheme an' he straight away went to Bathsheeber and told her what Adonijer was up to. Well, Bathsheeber went to David and reminded him of his promise, while Nathan popped in with the news that Adonijer was out on some hill callin' himself a king.

"David got pretty hot under the collar, but he went to action quickern' a salesman what's stepped on a cranky hound. He told Nathan to anoint Solomon king, which carried more weight than jest some priest doin' it. Then he told Solomon to ride David's personal donkey, and to sit upon his personal throne.

"What a mess. On one end of town Adonijer was sayin' *he* was king, an' on t'other, Nathan was insistin' that *Solomon* was. The folks, they pretty quick threw their lot in with Nathan. It was an easy decision, fer though Adonijer had David's gener'l, Solomon had David's donkey. The king's donkey outweighs the king's gener'l ever' time, you understand, though sometimes it's hard to tell the differ'nce between 'em.

"Adonijer was porkin' out with his guests an' didn't even know about Solomon gettin' oiled. But then this kid popped in an' shouted, 'Solomon's bin named king, an' he's a-ridin' David's donkey!' Well, the guests emptied that place like congressmen declarin' recess.

"Poor Adonijer. He'd made himself a vile thing in his brother's eyes. Lucky fer him, Solomon was in good spirits—bein' *under* the Spirit, you understand—an' Solomon let 'im go on a promise of good behavior.

"Even now Adonijer didn't accept his place in the scheme of things. He set his eyes on Abishag, a very pretty lady with a very ugly name. She had been David's companion in his final days, an' Adonijer figgered if he could have her as a wife, then the people would think of David when they saw her, an' so they would think of David when they saw him. But Solomon, he heard about this plan, an' so he dispatched Adonijer off t' feed the worms—if you know what I mean.

"If Adonijer had *only* sought the Almighty, things could've gone *so* easy.

"So! As I have said before, I will jus' tell you this, an' this alone: go ask th' good Lord. An' if it's okay with him, well . . . whatcha do is A-okay with me."

*END*

*This skit was inspired by Mark Twain's classic tale of* The Jumping Frog of Calaveras County. *You might have your actor read that piece aloud as a means of teaching him/her a voice and attitude.*

# 5

# A MATTER OF WORTH

"But store up for yourselves treaures in heaven, where moth and rust do not destroy, and where thieves do not break in and steal. For where your treasure is, there your heart will be also. . . . You cannot serve both God and Money" (Matt. 6:20, 21, 24b).

All those "prosperity gospel" preachers! They tell us God's greatest desire is that we become rich. They tell us we'll become wealthy if we "act on faith" by sending them money—lots of it—more than we can afford. Why? So they can continue to stay on the air, telling us to "act on faith" and send more money!

As a young lady I know often says, "What is wrong with this picture?"

From the Old Testament through the New, God constantly warns us to shun greed, to not "lay up treasures on earth" or use his name as a means of personal gain. How can these preachers open their Bibles and not see that? Jesus wants us to build up a wealth of faith, love, and humility—not dollars, bank accounts, and limousines.

Gehazi (see 2 Kings 5:1–27) was caught up in the notion of getting rich on God. His master, Elisha, believed God's approval and his own inner peace were enough. So tell me: if God wants us all to be rich, why do we honor Elisha and vilify Gehazi? And why did that faithless servant get punished for seeking financial "blessings?"

\* \* \*

Characters:
  GEHAZI, Friendly, laid-back, nonchalant.

ELISHA, Serious, severe, but holy.
NAAMAN, Hot-tempered but thankful.

*For a list of props, see index, page 166.*

## SCENE ONE

*Gehazi, broom in arm, is snoozing in a chair, leaning it back on its two legs. Elisha, a man with booming presence, enters.*

ELISHA   Gehazi!!

*Gehazi awakes with a start and the chair tumbles backward with him in it. He climbs under the chair and peers up guiltily.*

GEHAZI   Gracious greetings, O lord Elisha!

ELISHA   What are you doing!

GEHAZI   Why, looking at all the dust under here. Shame to your housekeeper, who just happens to be me. I'll do better. Really I will.

ELISHA   *[Considering him]* I have a message for you to send to King Joram. He's about to be distraught. The King of Aram is sending him a general named Naaman to be healed of leprosy. Joram is going to think that Aramite is trying to pick a fight.

GEHAZI   *[Taking the letter, which is on a scroll]* And this is a letter of comfort?

ELISHA   A letter of insult, really.

*Gehazi laughs good-naturedly, wagging his finger at Elisha as if to say, "Good joke! You got me!" However, Elisha only glares back until Gehazi, embarrassed, raises his other finger and claps his hands distractedly. Elisha exits. Gehazi turns to the audience.*

GEHAZI   It's all a matter of worth and I shouldn't complain. After all, I'm the servant of the great prophet Elisha! Everyone loves me. Or else.

I am overworked. Really I am. I sweep, I clean, I run these silly errands. But I was born to injustice, so I don't complain. And I must admit, I'm fed. I have clothes. I'm close to God. Whenever I'm close to Elisha, at least. And besides, it's a position with a future. I mean, when Elijah was around, my master was *his* servant—and look what it did for him!

I could do with an occasional smile. A little thanks now and then. But I don't mind. Really I don't. My life is hard, but I won't complain.

But we should be living like kings. Look at us: we live in a hut. We eat common food. I have one suit. Is this the way for a famous man of God and his loyal servant to live? Oh, we have the people's love and respect.

But wouldn't it be nicer to have their money?

After all, the servant is worth his wages. And when you work for God, when you're the biggest prophet in the land, it's only right that you should be filthy rich.

Take this message: "Why have you torn your robes? Have the man come to me and he will know that there is a prophet in Israel." No mention of money.  A tax-deductible gift. A few baubles to make life pleasant—some furs, a nice chariot and driver, an air conditioner for the dog.

Elisha's too self-sacrificial, and that's not what religion is about. Poor, misled Elisha. If only he'd allow me to barter for the creature comforts we men of God deserve.

*He exits.*

## SCENE TWO

*Naaman enters. He is huge, in armor, looking decidedly unfriendly. His hand is leprous, covered with white. He reads a sign.*

NAAMAN   "Elisha, Esquire, Man of God." *[To audience]* Joram was right. There *is* a man of God in Israel.

*He turns his back to the audience and knocks on the door (an imaginary door, likely, and if so, Naaman should stomp the floor with each knock). Gehazi enters.*

GEHAZI   Who are you to disturb the great and mighty Elisha! *[He suddenly notices whom he is scolding.]* Ooop! You must be Naaman. I like the double "A" in your name. Father's idea?

NAAMAN   *[Lifting him by the collar]* Is this the house of Elisha the prophet?

GEHAZI   In the spirit! *[Wagging a finger at him]* Ha, ha, ha!

NAAMAN   GRRRRR!

GEHAZI   [Again clapping distractedly] Ethnic humor! You wouldn't understand. Let's put me on the ground so my little feet will work and I'll go and get Elisha. [He exits.]

NAAMAN   I love it. He'll come out with trumpets! Shouting! He'll take the beautiful gifts I've brought! He'll make a mighty prayer, and lightning and thunder will strike me, filling me with the mighty healing power of his God!

GEHAZI   [Entering, looking disappointed] I have a message.

NAAMAN   And Elisha?

GEHAZI   [Smiling nervously] No. Just this message. [Now cringing] Go soak yourself.

NAAMAN   [Hauling him up again] WHAT!!!

GEHAZI   [Frantically] In the Jordan River! Seven times! Then your flesh will be restored! Then you will be cleansed! End of message. Please let go.

NAAMAN   [Dropping him] Of all the stupid plans!

He storms off as Gehazi watches, waving.

GEHAZI   Thank you for coming! Have a nice bath! Watch out for turtles! And, when you're healed and thanking our God, don't forget to . . . [Making a money symbol with his hand] thank us!

[To the audience:] Did you see his hand? [shudders] And he touched me with it! He's mad now, but he'll be back. I know the type. Generals! He'll yell and fume, but then he'll do it. He'll be overwhelmed with thanksgiving, and then he'll come back, praising God and Elisha—never little Gehazi, mind you. But I was born for it. I can wait.

[Rapturously:] But did you see his gold? Did you see those chariots? The horses? The servants? The little air conditioner with the doggy stenciled on? Did you see those fabulous robes and clothes? We'll live like kings!

We're God's servants! We're worth it! God wants us to be rich. But it won't happen. Not while Elisha's in charge. Such shortsighted men are my burden to bear.

## SCENE THREE

Gehazi is whittling. Enter Naaman, his hand cleansed. He is thrilled.

NAAMAN   I'm clean! I'm clean! Bring me the man of God!

GEHAZI   I'm sorry, he's indisposed. But if you'd like to leave a gift . . .

ELISHA   [Entering] Ah! You're healed! See what obedience to Jehovah brings!

GEHAZI   [Disappointed] I guess he's disposed after all.

NAAMAN   Now I know that there is no God in all the world except in Israel! Please accept a gift from your servant!

GEHAZI   Servant! Master, we're filthy rich! I mean, God's blessed us richly!

Elisha considers Gehazi a moment and turns to Naaman.

ELISHA   No.

33

NAAMAN & GEHAZI    No?

NAAMAN    If you took something, I'd be honored!

GEHAZI    That means he'd be insulted if we don't.

ELISHA    [Ignoring Gehazi] I honor God, not men.

NAAMAN    [Polite, but pressing] I feel I should give it.

GEHAZI    God *told* him to do this. Who are we to deny God's will?

ELISHA    God sustains us. We do not need it.

NAAMAN    [Insistent] Take it. It's nothing!

GEHAZI    [Frantic] It's EV-RY-THING!!

ELISHA    As surely as the Lord lives, whom I serve, I will not accept a thing.

NAAMAN    Okay!

GEHAZI    [Wailing] Oh, no!

NAAMAN    But if you won't, please let me, your servant, be given as much earth as a pair of mules can carry, for your servant will never again make sacrifices to any other god but the Lord.

ELISHA    [Happily, gently] Do so. And go in peace. [Slapping Gehazi on the back as Naaman exits] God's kingdom has been increased! Now there is true payment for the work of the Lord! [Happily, he exits.]

GEHAZI    We could have at least charged him for the dirt.

## SCENE FOUR

GEHAZI *enters with a handful of ritzy-looking robes.*

GEHAZI    [To audience] Elisha is right: we work for the kingdom. It's a matter of worth: the streets of heaven are paved with gold. [Whipping out two lumps of gold] And I've got two of the cobblestones.

[He puts them in his pockets, and is suddenly full of mock-repentance.] All right! I have sinned! You see a broken man! I couldn't resist! When the master went inside, I ran after Naaman.

All I could think of was his wealth—that he wanted to give to me!—and I couldn't resist! I told him, "My master has sent me to say, 'Two young prophets have just arrived from Ephraim. They are poor. Please give them each a talent of silver and a set of clothes.'" [Frantically:] I repent of my lie!

[Suddenly cool:] But if you think I'm repenting of taking the gifts, you're crazy. It's a matter of worth. We earned it. Besides, he *wanted* to give it! We're important servants of God. God wants us to be wealthy and he understands why I did it. He knows where my heart is in this matter. As to the lying, I promise never to do it again.

*Suddenly Elisha enters, full of wrath.*

ELISHA    **GEHAZI, WHERE HAVE YOU BEEN!!!**

*With a squeal, Gehazi frantically begins shoving the robes into his own robe. He answers with a squeak:*

GEHAZI    Right here all this time!

34

ELISHA   Wasn't my spirit with you when he got down from his chariot to meet you? Was this the time to take money and robes? God will deal with you for this!

*He exits in a storm. Gehazi waits for lightning to strike, burying his hands in his robe as he draws himself tight, but it doesn't come. Slowly, he regains his composure.*

GEHAZI   Well. Ha, ha. I told you God would understand. Naaman was thankful to me for his healing, and well he should be. And he gave his wealth to God's glory. I didn't twist his arm. If it hadn't been for me, he would never have taken that fateful bath. I only took what I deserved. God knows my heart. And so what Naaman gave to God, God turned around and gave to me!

*He raises up his hands, bringing them out of his cloak, to drive home his point. But he stares at those hands in shock for now they are leprous, white as snow!*

*END*

# 6

# THE PUPPET MASTER

"Then Judas Iscariot, one of the Twelve, went to the chief priests to betray Jesus to them" (Mark 14:10).

I once read that all people—good and bad—look on their lives as a movie, and that they all cast themselves as the heroes of the tale. As fallen people we rationalize our evil actions, blaming others for the wrong we ourselves do. I have done it—you have done it—Judas did it.

I doubt Judas looked on himself as evil when he betrayed Christ. He was getting vengeance for what he perceived as a wrong done against him. He acted on impulse, gave in to the temptations of Satan, and rather than seeking God he sought his own personal vindication for his act. The thoughts that might have led him to his betrayal are the subject of this one-act play.

For a while, Judas thought he got away with his act. If we aren't caught in our sins by others we may start out feeling that way too. But God has supplied each of us with a conscience; its purpose is to tell our hearts when the brain is playing games. It begins to pry away our self-protecting layers of lies and we see our own evil.

Here is where the grace of God kicks in. If we accept our responsibility and take it to him, he forgives us. And if we don't? Then there are two alternatives. One is to rebuild the layer of lies, and keep rebuilding it every time our consciences tear it down until we become so hardened that our consciences no longer bother us. Eventually we no longer feel bad for what we do. The price of this method is to live a constant lie and to forfeit our souls.

The other alternative is to become so guilt ridden we are simply driven to despair.

Forgiveness, hard-heartedness, or despair? Judas chose the latter. What about you?

\* \* \*

*Characters:*
CAIAPHAS
ANANIAS
PUPPET MASTER
2 WOMEN
JESUS
2 or 3 DISCIPLES (Optional)

This is a stylized play, with parts of it in prose and parts in rhyme. The trick to speaking rhyme on stage is to do it as though it is straight prose—without pausing or emphasizing the end of each stanza or rhyming word.

Dress the Puppet Master—Satan—in dark clothing, and give him facial makeup, if you can, as follows: quarter his face. Make the upper right and lower left hemispheres red, highlighting his eyebrows and lips in black. Make the upper left and lower right hemispheres black, using the red (or white) to highlight. Puppet Master might be played by either a man or a woman. He keeps a pair of those sticks that puppeteers use to control their marionettes, and at times he holds them over characters, as if manipulating them. His voice is always low and hissing—as though it is a sound we hear in our minds. Throughout, only the audience is aware of his presence. When Judas responds to him, it is as though he is answering thoughts in his own mind.

There should be a row of chairs upstage, and from that row of chairs the Puppet Master does his stuff.

Judas enters and crosses the stage, brooding. He sits and remains unmoving, still brooding. PM enters and climbs onto the chair. Enter Caiaphas and Ananias.

Alternative: for simplicity have Puppet Master's and Jesus' lines read offstage. In this case, eliminate the two or three disciples.

CAI   Then it is decided, Ananias. He must be eliminated.

ANAN   Yes, Caiaphas. But Jesus is too popular, so we must convince Rome to do the work for us.

CAI   Pilate will do it. He's in such trouble with Rome and so fearful of riots that he won't dare let Jesus go. Not if we demand a crucifixion.

ANAN   Our problem comes in choosing the right time to arrest him.

CAI   Pshaw! We could seize him anytime!

ANAN   And incite the crowds against us?

CAI   Then we'll have to find him when he's alone—or nearly so.

ANAN   If only we had inside help.

CAI   A betrayer?

ANAN   Yes. Someone who saw things the way we do. If only we could find someone who would understand. . . .

CAI   Yes! Who would understand. . . .

*PM has been manipulating them with his controls. As they exit, he squats and motions toward Judas—a fluid, dance-like motion. As he does he repeats Caiaphas' closing line, not missing a beat, and Judas picks up the line from him, as he rises to his feet.*

PM   Who would understand . . .

JUDAS   Who would understand . . . who would understand. . . .

Who would understand that this kingdom you speak of is not in this land? It's up in the sky! Jesus! You've treated me grand: You've given me power and purse strings but now—Oh you pitiful man! I see there's no nation or army that Judas Iscariot will ever command!

It could have been, you know. It could have been!

But it isn't, is it? No, you'll set no throne in Jerusalem, will you? "My kingdom is coming!" you told us, oh, how many times? "The kingdom is like a merchant who finds a valuable pearl!" And we believed for three years while you tromped about, gaining the support of the people—for what king can overthrow the conquerors if the people don't stand behind him? Of course that wasn't what you were building them for. You told us the truth, but you hid it in questions and parables, didn't you? We never knew what you really meant by a kingdom, did we? I do now, though I doubt if the others have caught on yet. They still see you like I did before: seated on your gilded throne, the emperor of Rome bound and at your feet, and each of us your ministers of state—me, in the treasury, watching it grow . . .

But that kingdom won't come!
No, that kingdom won't be!

Lord, this kingdom you vaunt
Is no kingdom I want—
I've a more mortal need!

PM   [Who has been watching with interest] Shall we call it greed?

JUDAS   Give to the poor and give and give and give until we're poor ourselves. Love your enemies. Forgive your brother. Man cannot live by bread alone. A kingdom . . . in heaven. A kingdom . . . of the spirit. All very nice. But a brother's hug does little for his place in society.

Jesus! You could rule this land! But instead, you've set your eye to spiritual things and a kingdom on the other side of the grave. That's all well and good for you, but why didn't you tell us that when you recruited us? I loved you, Jesus, but you've deceived me!

But still I love you.

PM   Or you did.

JUDAS   Or I did.

PM   Ha, ha, ha!

JUDAS   Yet for three years I followed you. I hung on every word.

PM   Three years is a good long time to be deceived.

JUDAS   Yet those three years you deceived me!

PM   You were going to be the treasurer. You were going to have more wealth than the merchants of Phoenicia!

JUDAS   You were going to be king. And I was going to be rich as one.

PM   And now look where he's brought you!

JUDAS   You deceived me!

PM   Ha, ha, ha!

JUDAS   Still, you're my friend.

PM   Look what he's brought you. Angry crowds. The Sanhedrin up in arms. Stirring up all that trouble. What do you think Rome will do? Better yet, what will you do?

JUDAS   Some friend. I should leave you!

PM   He's abused you!

JUDAS   You've used me, Jesus!

PM   And you'll just "leave" him? What about vengeance!

JUDAS   Nobody treats me this way!

PM   Ha, ha, ha!

JUDAS   But you're so good.

PM   Turn the other cheek? That's not the way of a man.

JUDAS   I want to get even!

PM   Betray him!

JUDAS   I know! I'll steal from the treasury.

PM   You've been doing that all along.

JUDAS   I'll take everything we have and leave.

PM   And what will the other disciples say?

39

JUDAS   "He was a thief, and we're glad he's gone."

PM   They've been suspicious of you all along.

JUDAS   They've always looked on me as an outsider. They've never trusted me.

PM   *[Sarcastically]* Can anything good come from Judas?

JUDAS   No wonder I've taken some funds for myself!

PM   Behold your friends: One deceiver, eleven despisers.

JUDAS   I want to get back at them all! Let them keep track of their own funds! I'll leave them— I'll do it tonight!

PM   What a blow! Do you think they'll miss you?

JUDAS   What good would that do? They can get by without me.

PM   Then think! Who can't they get by without?

JUDAS   I can . . . ! *[He stops, realizing the horror of his thought.]*

PM   Yes!

JUDAS   No.

PM   Turn him over to them!

JUDAS   He *was* my friend!

PM   Turn him over to me!

JUDAS   It's unthinkable!

PM   Judasssssssssss!

JUDAS   There must be another way!

PM   *[He states the following lines viciously:]* He deceived you!

JUDAS   I'm . . . going mad.

PM   For three years you've followed him!

JUDAS   But I won't let madness blind me!

PM   Now he's left you destitute!

JUDAS   I hate him!

PM   And the disciples don't trust you at all!

JUDAS   I hate them *all*!

PM   Jesus has made a fool of you.

JUDAS   I want to kill him!

PM   Ha, ha, ha! So what will you do?

JUDAS   I must think.

*He sits. The PM, exasperated, nearly dances around him, and Judas seems to hear his words.*

PM   I am the Puppet Master! Be
amazed! Be afraid! Be proud!
Listen to my words, a cloud
of rationalities and reasons
to perform a treason
on this King, this Lord, this
    Christ!
Look about you, Judassss!
There are ways you can
shake him from your cloak, sir,
rid yourself of this burr,
wash him from this city!

Won't that be so pretty
to your wounded ego?
There's one way, you know!

*He turns and works his controls as two women enter, talking.*

W. 1    Did you hear that Master Caiaphas is looking to find Jesus of Nazareth alone?

W. 2    *[Laughing]* Yes! He'd pay money for someone to show him how!

*They pass the two and exit. Jesus enters from another direction, followed by one or two disciples.*

JESUS    The kingdom of heaven is like a net which was thrown into the sea and gathered fish of every kind. When it was full, men drew it ashore and sat down and sorted the good into vessels but threw away the bad. So it will be at the close of the age. The angels will come out and separate the evil from the righteous, and throw them into the furnace of fire; and there men will weep and gnash their teeth. *[Significantly, to Judas:]* Do you understand all this?

JUDAS    You know I do.

*Jesus and disciples exit. Judas thinks a moment, and PM raises his controls again—for the first time using them on Judas.*

JUDAS    I feel alone.
I feel that, Jesus, you are
not the man you said.
Perhaps it's best for all of us
if Rome should have your head;
should have your body hanging from a tree!

It's cruel, but right:
the kingdom that you told us of
won't be here tonight.

The courts are out to get us.
They think that we are fools!
You cannot fight the Romans
healing blind men at a pool!
And now I know this kingdom
that glimmers in your eye
isn't here on earth at all:
It's somewhere in the sky.
And I must wait to rule in it
until I drop and die.
The people say we're freaks,
and it seems that you're too meek
to turn our foes into our hands.
And so . . . I'll turn you into theirs.

BOTH    I'll turn you into theirs!

*They flee. But Jesus enters the audience from the aisle, and he speaks encouragingly to them:*

JESUS    You will weep and lament, but the world will rejoice. You will be sorrowful, but your sorrow will then turn to joy! When a woman is in travail she has sorrow, because her hour has come. But when she delivers her child, she no longer remembers the anguish for joy of the child she has brought into the world. The hour is coming—indeed, it has come—when you will be scattered, every man to his home, and you will leave me alone. Yet, I am not alone, for the Father is with me. In the world you must have tribulations. But be happy! I have overcome the world!

*END*

# PART TWO

## The
## Daniel Skits

# INTRO

## THE DANIEL SKITS

Here are some fun (and weird) skits for a youth group—the Daniel skits, six separate stories from the first six chapters of that book in the Bible.

Each skit requires from six to twelve actors, a fair number of parts for your youth. While there are two or three roles with a fair chunk of lines, there are several parts that are loaded with short, easy one-liners, and of course you can always let your narrator cheat and read his/her part.

Any of these skits can be performed alone. If you feel really ambitious, you can try to tackle all of them as a show or fund-raiser. Go ahead; live dangerously. Casting refers to males for the most part, but nearly every role can be played by women as well.

The key to this collection is outlandishness. Keep the props simple and pretty stupid looking. The kings wander around armed with Whiffle® Bats, the lions' den and fiery furnace are made of cardboard boxes crudely painted. The rest of the set is made up of chairs and small tables—talk about inexpensive!

How should these parts be acted? Here's a hint: does Larry, Moe, and Curly ring a bell? How about the Monkees? Steve Martin? Mild lunacy is the order of the day and low humor reigns. One-liners, gags, silly rhymes. Let the actors ham it up. Really encourage ensemble acting, where everyone works together. When two or more actors work together (such as the Chaldeans in *The Fiery Furnace* or the magicians in *The King's Dream*), encourage some Monkees-style banter and movement. Nearly every part is a character part (even the narrator) and gives an opportunity for loads of fun.

Here are the plays and their corresponding chapters in the Book of Daniel:

- The Friends Who Obeyed God (ch. 1)
- The King's Dream (ch. 2)
- The Fiery Furnace (ch. 3)
- The Dream of the Tree (ch. 4)
- The Handwriting on the Wall (ch. 5)
- The Lions' Den (ch. 6)

# 7

# DANIEL 1:
# THE FRIENDS WHO OBEYED GOD

"But Daniel resolved not to defile himself" (Dan. 1:8a).

In an alien land where being disagreeable could arguably cost you your life, Daniel refused to bend. He was not going to compromise his beliefs and allow himself to be absorbed into the Babylonian culture. Threats didn't do it. The peer pressure from other captives giving in couldn't change his mind. Even guilt tactics from his apparent friend, Ashpenaz, were incapable of swaying his resolve.

Daniel and his friends refused to defile themselves with the Babylonian diet and, although they were undoubtedly ridiculed, they stuck to their guns. In the end they earned the respect and admiration of a kingdom.

There are two important lessons for youth in the first chapter of Daniel: first, don't give in to the pressure of worldly peers; if you stand by God, he'll stand by you. Ultimately, you're going to win. Second, standing up to peer pressure is a lot easier when you have Christian friends to lean on, and who are standing right beside you!

* * *

*Characters:* 6-9 actors.
   NARRATOR, who may double as . . .
   ASHPENAZ, servant of . . .
   NEBUCHADNEZZAR, who has
      conquered . . .
JEHOIAKIM, who also has a very
   small part. Also . . .
DANIEL
SHADRACH
MESHACH
ABEDNEGO
EMCEE, who may be played by
   the same guy as NEB or JEH.

*Props:*
   Whiffle® Bat (NEB); notepad and pen
   (ASH); 3 blank name tags and marker
   (NAR).

   A minimum set of a table and a few chairs.

*Narrator steps out.*

NAR   God created the heavens and the earth in six days, and on the seventh day he rested. But after that he selected his chosen people, and we never read of him resting again. I mean, they were always getting into trouble, and God was always having to get them out. First, the Israelites complained that they were slaves. So God delivered them out of Egypt. But they were so ungrateful that God ended up having to make them wander in the desert for 40 years. Then, he gave them the Promised Land. But again they disobeyed—worshiped other gods and lived immoral lives—so God let the people who made those other gods rule the Israelites. Then the people repented and cried out to God. He saved them. They'd fall away. He'd punish them. They'd repent. He'd save them. They'd fall away. And so on. This went on and on, back and forth, until God got really fed up. At last, he decided enough was enough, and so he let the king of Babylon . . .

*At this, narrator motions to Nebuchadnezzar, who has trotted in and stands proudly, bowing. Narrator waits a moment, and finally cues him.*

NAR   Introduce yourself, your highness.

NEB   Ooh! I'm Nebachazeddar! Nebuchacheddar! Bezzachananar! Neckaba . . . ! I'M ME!

NAR   Nebuchadnezzar. Anyway, God let the Babylonian king defeat the king of Jerusalem, who was . . .

JEH   *[Making a grand entrance]* Jehoiakim!

NEB   You are?

JEH   You bet!

NEB   Oh, goody!

*He whops Jehoiakim with a Whiffle® Bat and the Israelite sinks to the ground. Other players drag the poor fellow out.*

NAR   Now that he was top dog, the king decided to bring the wisest people of Israel . . .

NEB   Hey! Hey! Hey! Let me tell it!

NAR   Be my guest.

NEB   *[Calling]* Oh, Ashpenaz!!!

ASH   Oh, yethhir! Yethhir!

NEB   Take a letter.

ASH   Exth.

NEB   No!

ASH   Q?

NEB   I mean, write a letter!

ASH   Oh!

NEB   *[Pacing as he dictates]* "To my new subjects in Israel: send some of your people, both of the royal family and the nobility, youths without blemish . . .

ASH   *[Aside]* That means without zits.

NEB   . . . handsome and skillful in all wisdom, endowed with knowledge, understanding, and the ability to say my name!"

ASH   Your name, thir?

NEB   You know! Nezapu . . . Nechada . . . MY NAME! And, uh, when they arrive, teach them our laws and our language, so they can serve me. Oh! And while you're at it, give them a daily portion of rich food and wine, so we can fatten them up a bit. Got it?

ASH   Got it!

NEB   *[Suspicious]* You've . . . written the letter?

ASH   Of courth I have!

NEB   Then read it back to me.

ASH   *[Proudly]* "Double-yoo!"

NEB    [Chasing him away] AUUGGGGHHH!!!

NAR    And so some Israelites were brought to Babylon.

*Shadrach, Meshach, Abednego, and Daniel enter.*

NAR    One, of course, was Daniel. And the others . . .

SHAD    [Á la Three Stooges] Hello!

MESH    Hello!

ABED    Hello!

ALL 3    HELLO!

NAR    Can you guess their names?

*Narrator writes name tags and hands them out.*

NAR    Shadrach, Meshach, and Abednego!

ALL 3    [Embarrassed] Oh, right! I knew that.

NAR    For three years, Daniel and his friends went to school.

THE 4    Yuck!

NAR    And Ashpenaz saw to it that they got all kinds of food to eat.

*The four sit.*

DANIEL    Look at this stuff! Rib roast, T-bone, mashed potatoes!

SHAD    Banana splits, sundaes, stuffed tomatoes!

MESH    Big Macs, Whoppers! Crisp french fries!

ABED    Chocolate fudge and apple pie!

ALL 4    Yuck!

DANIEL    Ashpenaz!

ASH    [Hurrying on] Oh, yethhirs! Yethhirs!

DANIEL    We can't eat this stuff.

ASH    Why not?

DANIEL    Our God wants us to eat things that are good for us.

ASH    Like what?

SHAD    Like . . . cauliflower!

MESH    Beets!

ABED    Broccoli!

DANIEL    Spinach and stewed carrots!

ALL 4    Mmmmmmm!

ASH    I can't let you do that. It'th dithguthting. Here, eat thith.

DANIEL    But, why?

ASH    We need to fatten you up. You thee, if you jutht eat vegetablth, you'll look thkinny and really groth, and the king will get all upthet and he'll get mad at me and run me through with a thword, and then I'll be upthet, because *I'll* look really groth, and . . . !

DANIEL    Okay! Okay! Tell you what: let us eat veggies for ten days. Then, compare us with some of the guys who get to eat this . . . stuff. If we don't look better than them, we'll eat whatever you want.

ASH    What maketh you tho thure thith'll work?

49

DANIEL   We trust in our God.

NAR   So the test began. While the others had Cap'n Crunch and Lucky Charms for breakfast, Daniel and his friends ate Shredded Wheat.

ALL 4   Shredded Wheat! Boy, that's neat!

NAR   And, at lunchtime, the others had toasted cheese sandwiches, potato chips, and chocolate cake. Our friends had . . . cabbage.

ALL 4   When it comes to cabbage, we get savage!

NAR   At suppertime, the others had roast turkey, Jell-O, and pumpkin pie. These guys had . . . rutabagas!

*Again, the four tense to pop off some rhyme, but they stop, stumped. They look at one another, then huddle, mumbling. Suddenly they all sit straight again, grinning.*

ALL 4   We eat a rutabaga while we drive our Studebaga!

NAR   Ten days passed.

MESH   Boy, that was quick.

NAR   And the time arrived for the big test.

*Enter the EMCEE, grinning.*

EMCEE   We're playing a joke on Mr. Ashpenaz! We're taking the fatteners out of his family's diet!

ASH   *[Frantic]* Oh! You can't do that! I depend on thothe fattenerth! You put them back! Oh! I'll declare war! I'll . . . ! Oh!

EMCEE   *[Aside]* Actually, we're only teasing! Because there *are* fatteners in these boys' diets. You see, they're just in the form of vegetable nutrients! *[To Ashpenaz]* Now, Mr. Ashpenaz, we're going to compare someone eating the old fatteners against your family, with those old junk food fatteners removed.

*He selects someone from the audience and lines him or her up with Abednego. Ashpenaz compares their waists.*

ASH   I don't believe it! Thith one ith *definitely* wider.

ABED   Why do I suddenly feel like doing laundry?

NAR   Yes, they were definitely healthier, and so the four friends were allowed to continue their diet, which God wanted them to follow. And God blessed them, and they became wiser and stronger than any of the king's men—especially Daniel, who became ten times better than all the magicians in the kingdom! So, if you know God wants you to do something, do it! Even if everyone you know is doing something else, and you're afraid they might laugh at you. Because, when we do what God wants us to, he blesses us, and makes us happier than those guys could ever be.

*END*

# 8

# DANIEL 2: THE KING'S DREAM

"He reveals deep and hidden things; he knows what lies in darkness, and light dwells with him" (Dan. 2:22).

It took a captive from a foreign land to teach the great and mighty King Nebuchadnezzar that all mysteries are known to God and that light—that is, true understanding—comes directly from the Lord.

The king had a disturbing dream, and he wanted answers as to what it meant. Just as we are doing more and more today, he turned to the occult for answers. Many kings would have accepted whatever the wizards would have told them, but Nebuchadnezzar, to his credit, was honestly seeking the truth. He put the wizards to the test to see if they really knew what they were talking about. "*You* tell *me* my dream!" he challenged. When they couldn't, he destroyed the false priests and turned to the Hebrew God.

When he saw that God proved true, he praised him.

The New Age isn't new. In fact, much of it is based on the ancient Babylonian religion! What it did for Nebuchadnezzar, it will do for you . . . absolutely nothing.

Turn to the only Truth that sets you free—Jesus.

\* \* \*

*Characters:* 6 or more actors.
  NARRATOR
  A PASSEL OF MAGICIANS (at least
    two—preferably more)

NEBUCHADNEZZAR
ARIOCH, a guard
DANIEL

*Props:*
  "Bogart" hat, trench coat and tommy gun or sword (ARIOCH); tablet on an easel or an overhead projector (DANIEL)

*Narrator steps out.*

NAR   Now God made Daniel ten times better than all the magicians in Nebuchadnezzar's kingdom. There came a time when that wisdom served Daniel well, for one day the king had a bad dream.

*Neb is sleeping, snoring like an ox. Suddenly he jumps up with a shriek.*

NEB   Woooow! You would not believe the dream I just had. I mean, it was worse than no summer vacation. There was this awful thing like . . . like . . . Darth Vader, only uglier, and . . . and . . . what did it mean? It must have meant *something.* Dreams always do! Maybe I could read about it in the *National Enquirer.* . . . No, that doesn't come out till next week. I gotta know now! Oh, what'll I do? I know! I'll call my magicians! MAGICIANS!

*The magicians scurry in, bowing, and grovelling. Finally one stands up.*

MAG 1   What is it, O mighty good one?

NEB   I've had a dream.

MAGICIANS   Oh wow, that's heavy, man.

NEB   I want you to interpret it.

*This sends the magicians into a frantic huddle. Finally they turn around and one addresses the king.*

MAG 2   So, King, live foreffer. You say you haff had zis dream, a repressed image in your mind. Vell! Der iss nothink for you to vorry about. You chust settle back und tell us dis dream, und ve shall tell you vot it means, ya?

*The king's response sends them into another squealing huddle, during which louder squeals are heard each time the king makes a point.*

NEB   You'll tell me what it means, alright! If you don't, I'll have you torn limb from limb, and your houses will be laid in ruins! But . . . ? *[Sweetly]* If you can tell me my dream and its interpretation, I shall give you gifts and rewards and great honor. Therefore, show me the dream and its meaning.

MAG 3   Oh, mighty good one, may you live forever. . . .

MAGICIANS   And so on and so forth.

MAG 3   It's good you've said this and gotten it all, well, into the open. You've let it all hang out, as we might have said once upon a time and, well, that's just good for the soul, you know? I mean, we're having a little give! A little take! We understand each other and I

think, speaking for myself of course, that maybe we all feel better for it. What say, gang?

MAGICIANS   Oh, yeah, better. Much better.

MAG 3   But now we must get on to a level of purer understanding. In other words, you tell us the dream, and we'll tell you what it means.

NEB   Are you stalling for time?

MAGICIANS   *[Looking about innocently]* Who? US?

NEB   I think you are, because you know that if you can't tell me my dream, it's K-k-k-k-k-k! for you. So. YOU tell me the dream. That way, *I'll* know you can also show me its real meaning.

MAGICIANS   Oh, mighty king live forever!

NEB   And so on and so forth.

MAG 1   Nobody can do that!

MAG 2   Vot you tink ve are? Magick or somtink?

NEB   You *are* magicians.

MAG 3   But magicians can't tell dreams. It would take a god to do that!

NEB   RRRAAARRRGHGHGH!

*The magicians scatter.*

NAR   So the king, being a violent man, ordered that all the magicians and wise men in Babylon be torn limb from limb.

NEB   Hey, it's cheaper than unemployment.

NAR   And, if you'll remember, the wisest men in all of Babylon were Daniel, Shadrach,

Meshach, and Abednego. As you might guess, these guys were a little bit . . . concerned. So Daniel sought out Arioch, who was in charge of killing the wise men.

*Arioch enters, looking like a 30's hit man.*

ARIOCH   Crush. Kill. Destroy. Fold. Spindle. Mutilate.

DANIEL   Pssst! Arioch!

ARIOCH   A wise man!

DANIEL   Wait! Don't kill me! Truce! Truce!

ARIOCH   The king said t'kill all the wise men! Ha! Ha! *[He grabs Daniel.]* It wasn't very wise o' you t' come out here like . . . !

*He pauses to consider what he has just said.*

DANIEL   Aha!

ARIOCH   *[Releasing him]* Yer off the hook.

DANIEL   Good.

ARIOCH   But only till I find the error in me logic.

DANIEL   Why does the king want to kill us?

NAR   And Arioch explained.

ARIOCH   The king had this terrible dream, see?

DANIEL   I see.

ARIOCH   An' he wanted the magicians to tell 'im what it was, an' then tell 'im what it meant. He figured, if they could tell him what the dream was about, without him tellin' them first, then he could believe their interpretation, see?

DANIEL   I see. And if they couldn't?

ARIOCH   Then he was gonna tear 'em limb from limb. As it turned out, none of 'em could tell it! See?

DANIEL   *[Paling slightly]* I see. Then, if someone tells him his dream and what it means, he'll stop killing us?

ARIOCH   That's right. Takes a real wise man t' come up wit dat, Dan'l.

DANIEL   Thank you!

*They shake, but then it occurs to them what has just been said. Daniel makes a hasty escape with Arioch hot on his tail.*

NAR   Daniel knew what he had to do to save himself and his friends. Of course, he didn't have any better idea what the king had dreamed than anyone else, but he did have one big advantage over them: God.

DANIEL   *[Entering]* Tonight, we must pray and seek God's mercy, that he might show me the dream. And tomorrow I'll go and tell the king. *[He exits.]*

NAR   So Daniel and his friends prayed. And during the night the Lord did show Daniel the dream, in a vision, and Daniel awoke, praising God! He told the others, then he hurried to the king.

*Nebuchadnezzar enters, followed by Daniel.*

NEB   This better be good, Daniel.

DANIEL   Oh, it will be.

NEB   So. You can tell me my dream and its interpretation?

DANIEL   Not me, nor any man. But there is a God in heaven who knows everything, and reveals great mysteries to us. Through your dream he has told you what will happen in later days. And through God—not through any wisdom of my own—I will now tell you that dream and what it meant.

NAR   And what Daniel said truly amazed him.

DANIEL   [Using a visual aid—either paper pad on an easel or an overhead projector—as he speaks] In your dream, you saw a giant statue of a man. Its head was gold, its breast and arms were silver, its belly was bronze, its legs were iron, and its feet were part iron and part clay. Tacky, but effective. As you looked, a great stone struck the statue's feet of iron and clay, breaking them to pieces. Then the whole statue broke into tiny pieces that were blown away by the wind. Then the stone turned into a giant mountain that filled the whole world.

NEB   I am truly amazed.

NAR   [To audience] Told you.

DANIEL   You think that's good, wait'll you hear the interpretation! You, O king, are the head of gold. After you another kingdom will rise—it won't be as good as yours, and that's why it's made of silver. You know, the silver breast and arms.

NEB   Oh. Right.

DANIEL   Then, a third kingdom will rise. . . .

NEB   That's the bronze one!

DANIEL   Very good! And after that, a fourth one, as strong as iron! But! Remember that the feet were iron and clay? Well, the fourth kingdom will become divided, and as iron and clay is both strong and weak, so will this kingdom be both strong and weak. Again, iron and clay don't mix, and so the divided kingdom will never hold together. And in that day, God will set up a kingdom which will never be destroyed, and no one else shall ever rule over its people. It'll smash these other kingdoms and will last forever!

NEB   Forever!

DANIEL   The end.

NEB   Your God told you all that?

DANIEL   Every bit.

NEB   Then your God is the God of all gods and the Lord of all kings, for only you were able to reveal my dream!

NAR   And so the king made Daniel the ruler of the entire province of Babylon and, at Daniel's request, he appointed Shadrach, Meshach, and Abednego rulers as well. So you see: even the foolishness of God is greater than the wisdom of men.

*END*

# 9

# DANIEL 3: THE FIERY FURNACE

"If we are thrown into the blazing furnace, the God we serve is able to save us from it, and he will rescue us from your hand, O king. But even if he does not, we want you to know, O king, that we will not serve your gods or worship the image of gold you have set up" (Dan. 3:17–18).

How many of us can claim a faith like that of Shadrach, Meshach, and Abednego? They knew that God could free them even from the painful death promised by a fiery furnace. But—get this—they knew he might well choose to let the fires consume them. They decided it was worth the cost of following him.

It isn't easy, sometimes, to admit to friends that you do "Christian things" like going to church and reading your Bible, or that you don't want to listen to the perverse and violent lyrics in much of today's music. It isn't easy to trust and honor God when your friends are partying with kegs of beer and involving themselves in premarital sex which at first glance (and *only* first glance) seems so "cool."

With God's help and influence, you can follow him and still be popular, because a lot of your peers will respect the fact that you stand up for what you believe. Then again, maybe they won't. They just might dismiss you as a stodgy flake. What then?

Remember Daniel's friends, facing that fire, ready to pay any price.

\* \* \*

*Characters*: 8.
NARRATOR
2 CHALDEANS
NEBUCHADNEZZAR
FIRE, a guy in a yellow suit
SHADRACH
MESHACH
ABEDNEGO

*Props*:
Newspaper (CHAL 2); Whiffle® Bat (NEB); cue cards (CHAL 2).

You'll need a fiery furnace. This furnace could be an elaborate structure of porcelain with beautifully gilded trim and dials and levers and dry-ice smoke coming out of its roof, but if your budget comes in under $30,000, you might just settle for some tempera paints on a couple of refrigerator boxes, cut open and glued together instead.

*Narrator steps out.*

NAR   Old Nebuchadnezzar was a lot like the Hebrews. Remember how he praised God after Daniel interpreted his dream? It wasn't long before he'd slipped right back into his old habits.

55

NEB    I, Nebuchazizzle . . . Neversaynever . . . Nabochondroma . . . Nacho . . . I, YOUR KING! have made a golden image, 87 feet high and eight feet wide! Now, everyone in the kingdom must worship it, and whoever does not fall down and worship my image shall be thrown into a burning, fiery furnace! I'm such a devil!

NAR    There were some Chaldeans who didn't like Shadrach, Meshach, and Abednego because those Hebrew friends had such power. These Chaldeans wanted to find a way to get the Israelites out of office, so they could have the office themselves.

CHA 1    *[Entering]* . . . But you just can't catch these guys doing anything wrong!

CHA 2    *[Also entering, and reading a newspaper]* They're such goody-two-shoes!

CHA 1    Although the way they eat those spinach-and-broccoli pizzas is certainly a crime.

CHA 2    *[Noticing an item in the newspaper]* Wait! I think we've got them!

CHA 1    What! How!

CHA 2    Look: this article from Nebuchadnezzar says, "I, King What's-His-Face have made a golden image and everyone must worship it!"

CHA 1    So?

CHA 2    Don't you see? Shadrach, Meshach, and Abednego are followers of the God Jehovah. They'll *never* worship an image!

CHA 1    Big deal. So they get slapped with a fine.

CHA 2    Says here they'll get slapped into a fiery furnace.

*The two look at each other, victory in their faces.*

BOTH    **WE'VE GOT 'EM!!**

NAR    And so their enemies reported them to the king.

*Chaldean 1 hurries to Nebuchadnezzar and, childlike, hems and haws, then whispers in his ear.*

NEB    They do, huh? Izzat so?

*He crosses quickly to Shadrach, Meshach, and Abednego, who have just entered.*

NEB    Is this true?

SHAD    Is what true, Nebuchadnezzar?

NEB    *[To audience]* How come everyone else can say it? *[To Shad, very calmly:]* Is it true that you refuse to worship my golden image! Now look, I'm not a bad guy, and I know *you* aren't bad guys, so whatever you tell me, I'll take your word for it. If you say you *do* worship my golden image, well, hey, that's that. But if you say you won't, then you're throwing a monkey wrench into the whole works. That would get me just the tiniest bit angry, I do admit, and I would have to hit you with some trifling little punishment . . . like throwing you alive into a fiery furnace stoked to about a trillion degrees.

SHAD    Is that Fahrenheit, or Celsius?

MESH    Dear King . . .

NEB    *[Stopping him]* "Dear King." It's always bad news when they start out with "Dear King." This is bad news, isn't it?

ABED    There's really no need to answer you.

MESH    But, hey, why not?

SHAD    It's like this—if you throw us into your fiery furnace, the God we serve is able to deliver us from it.

MESH    And from you.

ABED    Even if he chooses not to save us, we still won't worship your image.

NEB    *[Boiling]* Oooh, that makes me so mad!

CHA 1    *[Rushing over]* Oh, may I throw them in the furnace, your highness? Can I? Can I?

NEB    *[Very polite]* Please do.

NAR    And so, the friends were bound and the guard led them to the fiery furnace. The king, meanwhile, was so mad that he made the furnace seven times hotter than usual. It was so hot, in fact, that the flames leaped out and killed the guard.

*The Chaldean opens the door just as the statement is made, and he turns in protest.*

CHA 1    Now, just a minute!

*But a Flame leaps out, screaming ghoulishly, and pulls him in.*

NAR    And the three friends were thrown in.

SHAD    After you.

MESH    No, no, after you.

ABED    Oh, no, I insist!

SHAD    Really, the first should be the one with the hardest name.

NEB    *[Sweetly]* Why don't you three go in together?

ABED    What a fine idea!

*And the three step into the furnace. Laughing wickedly, the king hurries to the door and looks in.*

NEB    Ha, ha, ha! That'll teach 'em! Wait a minute. They're just walking around in there. Now that just burns me up—they're not burning up! Just walking around, the four of them . . . !

*He does a double take and counts on his fingers.*

NEB    Shadrach, Meshach, Abedne . . . Shadrach, Meshach, Abed . . . ! *[He crosses to narrator.]* Didn't I throw three guys in there?

NAR    Could've sworn you did.

NEB    But . . . I just saw *four* men walking around in there, and they're not hurt . . . and the fourth one looked like a son of the gods . . . and . . . uh-oh.

*He hurries to the door, opens it. The Flame leaps out at him and he beats it back with a bat.*

NEB    Shadrach! Meshach! Abednego! Come on out! *[They do so.]* Your God has blessed you for your faithfulness! Because you trusted in him and refused to worship any other god, he sent his angel to protect you. Therefore, I will make a decree!

*He faces the audience. The surviving Chaldean rushes into the aisle with cue cards so that he may read the following speech:*

NEB    From the great king Nevercannever. . . Bezzachadreddar. . . Frazzlekadrazzle . . .

CAST    **NEBUCHADNEZZAR!**

57

NEB    To all the kingdom: These three men have been spared by the wonderful mercy and love of their God. We must all, then, be good to this God who is so full of those wonderful traits, love and mercy. Therefore, let no one say a word against this loving God or they shall be torn limb from limb and their houses shall be laid in ruins.

*Laughing and rubbing his hands together, he exits.*

NAR    So you see, loving God and standing up for him is worth any price because he loves you so.

*END*

# 10

# DANIEL 4: THE DREAM OF THE TREE

"Renounce your sins by doing what is right, and your wickedness by being kind to the oppressed. It may be that then your prosperity will continue" (Dan. 4:27b).

Nebuchadnezzar must have been a slow learner. Three times he'd seen the power of God, and while he picked up a pointer or two on each occasion, it still took a radical act on God's part to really straighten him up. His biggest problem was the same one that knocks so many of us for a loop: pride.

After a bout with a fiery furnace he learned to recognize God as one of the greatest beings around. But he refused to take second place to the Almighty, and that was an almighty big mistake.

God warned him through a dream to watch his step. Daniel was boldly honest in its interpretation: humble yourself. Pay attention to the people. If you don't quit looking at only yourself, you'll lose your sanity until the day you face up to God's proper place in your life.

The king didn't listen, and one day while he was glorifying himself on the castle ramparts, he was stricken with a madness that left him no better than the beasts of the field. It took seven years of living like that, but finally he humbled himself and even wrote an edict telling the world of God's glory and his own considerable lack of worth in comparison.

What will it take for you to give up your pride and admit that, without God, you're nothing more than "the flowers of the field" (1 Peter 1:24)?

\* \* \*

*Characters:* 8–12 actors. (Animals can double as magicians.)
NARRATOR
NEBUCHADNEZZAR
ASHPENAZ
PRUNER
TREE
ANIMALS (Fox, Turkey, Penguin)
MAGICIANS 1, 2, 3

*Props:*
Cue cards; glass of water, safari hat, pruning shears (PRUNER); bird, branches, apple, banana (TREE); water, an iron, an air horn (ASHPENAZ); feather (NEBUCHADNEZZAR).

*A bed—it can be two or three chairs with a blanket—is on stage, and NEB lays there snoring gently.*

*Narrator steps out.*

NAR   You may remember that Daniel was ten times smarter than all the wise men in Babylon. And you may remember that Daniel had proven himself by interpreting a dream Nebuchadnezzar once had about a statue made of different elements, which got swept away by the wind. You may further remember that Nebuchadnezzar made Daniel a real hero and announced that Daniel's God was the only God. You may also remember how fickle Nebuchadnezzar was. In a short time he was setting up statues of himself for people to worship, and Daniel's friends all showed him once again just who God was. And, once again, he proclaimed Jehovah from the housetops. Well, as the curtain opens, we find old Neb in love with himself again. And, we find God sending him another dream.

*Neb is lying on his bed, asleep. Strains of Nutcracker Suite are played as the dream commences:*

*First, a tree dances in. The tree is dressed in brown, holding branches in her hands and teeth. A bird roosts in her hair. She dusts Neb's face with one branch and he sits up, sneezing, and stares at the tree.*

NEB   Is that you, Marley?

TREE   Try again, Scrooge.

NEB   What are you?

TREE   A tree.

*Tree takes center stage. Neb crosses to it and looks it over.*

NEB   What a tree! What an enormous tree! What a fruitful tree!

TREE   *[Offering an apple]* Care for an apple?

NEB   I don't want an apple.

TREE   *[Offering a banana]* How about a banana?

NEB   Sure, I'll take a banana.

TREE   How appropriate.

*As he munches his banana, animals come in, each lying beneath the tree.*

TURKEY   I'm a turkey.

FOX   I'm a fox.

PENGUIN   I'm a penguin.

NEB   Why, look at this! There's room beneath this huge and fruity tree for all the animals of the field.

*Music stops. Pruner comes in, wearing a safari hat and carrying pruning shears.*

PRUNER   Excuse me. Are you Nebuchadnezzar?

NEB   Yes, I'm Nezzapa . . . Nemmana . . . I'm me.

PRUNER   Is this your dream?

NEB   So it would appear. Would you explain it?

PRUNER   No. But I do have a speech.

*He pulls out some paper and clears his throat. Ashpenaz enters, doing as he is commanded. He "Yeth thirs!" as he works.*

PRUNER   *[Overly dramatic]* Cut down this tree, and trim off its branches! Strip off its leaves…

TREE   *[Slapping Ashpenaz]* Don't you dare!

PRUNER   . . . and scatter its fruit! Chase the animals away! But leave the stump and the roots, and bind them with iron! *[Ashpenaz drapes a clothes iron over her.]*

*During all this, Neb has wandered over to watch the odd ceremony.*

PRUNER   Now Part Two of my speech. Let him be drenched with the dew of heaven!

*Ash throws a big glass of water on tree—and soaks Neb as well.*

PRUNER   Let him live with the animals and the plants of the earth!

TREE   I already am.

PRUNER   Let his mind be changed from that of a man to an animal.

*Tree makes a "crazy" face, babbling as she runs her finger back and forth across her lips and circling in the "nuts" fashion with her other hand.*

PRUNER   And let this occur for seven times seven times.

NEB   You're repeating yourself.

PRUNER   No, I'm not. Just think about it.

NEB   *[More confused than ever]* I'll try.

PRUNER   *[Going to tree]* And maybe now, young lady, you'll understand just who's Most High around here!

*All but Neb go into a freeze.*

NEB   Is that it?

*Tree, Ash, and Pruner all turn to Neb, say "Uh-huh!" while emphasizing each syllable with a finger. Then they all go back into their freeze.*

NEB   *[Nearly wailing as he sinks onto his bed]* But I don't understand!

TREE, ASH, PRUNER   That's *your* problem!

*They exit. Neb falls back, asleep. Ashpenaz re-enters with an air horn, toots it at Neb, who wakes up with a start.*

NEB   That is the strangest dream I've ever had.

*Enter the magicians.*

MAG 3   So, tell it to us, O mighty good one.

MAGICIANS   May you live forever!

MAG 1   And so on and so forth.

NARRATOR   So he did!

NEB   What do you think, guys?

MAG 2   Dot iss der strangest dream I have effer heard.

MAG 3   King, babe, may you forever . . .

MAGICIANS   Etcetera, etcetera.

MAG 3   We'll now apply our great psychological training to delve the depths of your mind and to tell you the very thing you most want to know.

NEB   *[Pleading]* Did my dream have a meaning?

*Magicians hold a brief huddle. Then, all at once:*

MAGICIANS   What do YOU think?

*There is a pause.*

MAG 2   Der explanation uff your dream iss simple. You dreamt that a tree came in, gave you a banana, and then some animals came and sat under it. Then a man came and shouted veird things about pruning branches and tying der tree in irons. Den dey threw water on it, und told it to go bonkers for seven years, und den it vould know chust who vass Most High, und who vass not!

NEB    I know that! What did it mean?

MAG 2    How should I know! It vas your dream, not mine!

NEB    GET OUT OF HERE!!!

NAR    And then he remembered Daniel, who had explained his earlier dream.

DANIEL    *[Entering]* So lay it on me.

NAR    So he did.

NEB    So what do you think?

DANIEL    Eww.

NEB    *[Worried]* Eww?

DANIEL    *[Nodding]* Eww.

NEB    Bad news?

DANIEL    Uh-huh.

NEB    *[Resigning himself]* Lay it on me.

DANIEL    The tree, O king, is you.

NEB    Eww.

DANIEL    Like you, it's grown big and bad and strong, and everyone rests beneath it. The messenger was delivering the commands of God, and the command is this: because you think of yourself as greater than him, he's going to remove your authority from you. He's going to make you go insane, until your hair grows like

feathers and your nails like claws, for seven years—until you finally fess up that he is Lord.

NEB    Double-eww. What can I do?

DANIEL    Confess your sins. Give up your bad attitude. Admit it took God to give you all you got! Is that so hard?

*He exits.*

NAR    And he followed Daniel's advice. For, say, five minutes?

NEB    Give me a break!

NAR    Okay. For a year. But one night Nebuchadnezzar was walking on the roof of his palace when he was overcome with awe.

NEB    Aww, look at this great place! Aww, look at how great Babylon looks! And I made it! I built it! I am full of mighty power and majesty!

*Enter pruner.*

PRUNER    Hi, there.

NEB    Aww, I shouldn't have said all that.

PRUNER    Poof.

NAR    Immediately the dream was fulfilled, and Nebuchadnezzar went around acting a little, well, nutsy. *[Neb now begins to run around acting like a loon.]* He was driven from the people and his hair grew like feathers, and his nails like claws. His body was drenched with the dew of heaven.

NEB    *[Stopping suddenly]* Come on! Not again!

*The Pruner enters and splashes a glass of water in Neb's face.*

NAR  For seven years Nebuchadnezzar lived like this, when suddenly, and at long last permanently, the king's sanity returned as he realized who was Lord.

NEB  Ho! Wait! Now I see it! *[Pulling a feather from his hair]* Where'd this feather come from? I'm nothing! I'm nobody! My kingdom's just a temporary thing, but the Lord's is eternal! It'll last from generation to generation. All the people of the earth—we're nothing! He does what he wants. *I* can't hold back his hand! Who am I to say, "What have you done?"

NAR  His advisors sought him out.

ASHPENAZ  There he ith!

NAR  And restored him to his throne, where he gave them the moral of this story.

*Neb sits at his throne and his subjects enter, including Daniel, the magicians and, if you've done any skits involving them, Shadrach, Meshach, and Abednego.*

NEB  I, Nebuchadredder … Nemanamemmer … NEBUCHADNEZZAR! Glorify the King of heaven, because everything he does is right and all his ways are just, and those who become too proud he can humble. *[All applaud. Neb raises his hand and draws it down, a victorious sign, as he gleefully shouts]* YES!!!

*END*

# 11

# DANIEL 5: THE HANDWRITING ON THE WALL

"You have been weighed on the scales and found wanting" (Dan. 5:27).

There's an old television sitcom about a matronly woman named Maude. She became famous for pointing a finger at her TV husband, melting him with a withering glare, and proclaiming, "God is going to get you for that!"

Our sins will certainly lead to judgment, but it isn't because God is out to "get" us. It's because we've foolishly "gotten" ourselves.

Belshazzar learned this lesson the hard way. He lived a life of mockery, lust, and greed. To show God what he thought of him, he partied with cups taken from Jerusalem's temple. In like manner, he ignored the needs of his own kingdom. God sent a special message of judgment, written on the plastered walls of Belshazzar's banquet hall: *Mene, mene, tekel, parsin.* It meant he'd been measured, found wanting, and that his kingdom would be split up and given to other men—that very night. These attacking armies weren't created miraculously from the dust about Babylon. They'd been taking advantage of the corrupt king's foolishness for many months. God simply lit the spark that delivered the death blow.

We also pay the price for our sins—judgment from God, but self-inflicted. We lifted a jacket at the department store and wound up wearing a police record. We gave in to the passion of the moment and contracted gonorrhea or worse. We told so many lies that no one believes us, or we betrayed a friend and we're no longer trusted. Even when we seem to escape detection of our sins by people, we must live with the realization of what we've done and someday answer to God.

When Nebuchadnezzar sinned, God gave him a warning. That meant he had a chance to mend his ways. Belshazzar wasn't given a choice. He was so caught up in his sin and his heart was so hardened against God that God simply sent a message, "It's all over. You're finished." The same can happen to you. Don't let your relationship with him erode to the point where your love completely dies. Repent and renew while you can!

\* \* \*

*Characters:* 9-12 actors.

  NARRATOR
  BELSHAZZAR
  ASHPENAZ
  DANIEL
  QUEEN
  A HAND
  MAGICIANS 1, 2, 3
  SOLDIER
  MEMBERS of COURT (optional)

*Magicians may double as soldier and hand. Ashpenaz can, if necessary, be cut from the script.*

*Props:*
 Golden cup, Whiffle® Bat (BELSHAZZAR);
 felt-tip marker (HAND); pointer (DANIEL);
 Whiffle® Bat (SOLDIER).

*A long table. Belshazzar, Queen, Ashpenaz, and possibly one or two other members of the court, sit behind it. They are heavily into some merrymaking, pantomiming eating and drinking, laughing and gabbing back and forth. In the midst of them is the narrator who addresses the audience. The only item on the table is a golden cup. There is a standing panel at Down Stage Left.*

NAR Nebuchadnezzar was a hard nut, but at least he knew when he'd been cracked. There were a few times when this strange king got a little arrogant, but always the Israelite Daniel or his friends would point out the error of the king's ways and—with a little dream or object lesson from God—he finally fessed up that the Lord is—*the Lord.* It was a shame his son didn't think that way. Yes, Belshazzar was hateful toward God—arrogant—rude—

BEL *[A loud hiccup]*

NAR And crude. *[To actor on his left]* Pass the fish.

BEL *[To his friends]* So Daddy-o kept this warped little Jewish guy on retainer, and he tells me to worship his God. So I says, "Hey, Daddy-o, Bel is my God, and I don't need to fear or worship some God from a country you conquered." That's why I brought all these neat dishes up from the Jewish temple, down in Jerusalem, so we could have our orgies with 'em and stick his holiness in his face!

*Suddenly, a hand rips through the lower part of the panel. It is holding a felt-tip marker, and it begins to write in big awkward letters: MENE, MENE, TEKEL, PARSIN. Belshazzar and all his guests gasp.*

BEL This is terrible!

QUEEN You're telling me. I just had that wall plastered yesterday.

BEL What could those words mean?

NAR It could have been the latest lyrics from a heavy metal track. But the only heavy metal in those days was forged and turned into swords and kettles. It could have been crude graffiti, but that wasn't likely—the kids weren't home from school yet. Finally someone concluded . . .

ASHPENAZ It mutht be the hand of a god.

*Belshazzar crosses to the writing.*

BEL "Mene, Mene, Tekel" and "Parsin." It must mean terrible things. Ashpenaz!

ASH Yeth, thir! Yeth, thir!

BEL Send a message to the magicians! Tell them anyone who can interpret this writing shall be clothed in purple, have a gold chain for his neck, and will be third in command to rule the kingdom!

*Ashpenaz rushes off, only to be stampeded and dragged back on by the magicians.*

MAG 1 Oh mighty good one!

MAGICIANS May you live forever!

MAG 2 Ve haff come to interpret this writink for you!

MAG 3 Stand back, babe, and let us do our stuff.

*They now line up to study the writing and do so, one at a time.*

MAG 1   OH NO!

BEL   Do you know what it says?

MAG 2   Yes! And it's terrible! Awful! What a terrible day is upon us!

BEL   What is it? What is it?

MAG 2   It's . . . it's . . . the new fall season on network TV!

*Angrily, Bel swats the magician with his Whiffle® Bat.*

NAR   Strike one.

MAG 2   This iss obviously a message from deep within your mind.

BEL   It isn't from Bel?

MAG 2   Uff course. But Bel is within you.

BEL   Here I thought it was indigestion.

MAG 2   He iss tellink you to change your ways!

BEL   You mean, give up my immorality? Face up to the enemy who's at my gates?

MAG 2   No! No! Uff course not! He vants you to chust forget about them, und to throw bigger parties. He also vants you to increase your magicians' salaries by fifty percent.

*Bel whops him.*

NAR   Strike two.

MAG 3   *[Eyeing bat]* I, uh . . . I'd love to interpret this, but I seem to have left my glasses at home.

BEL   Can't you idiots come up with anything!!

*The magicians huddle, making squealing noises. Finally they break apart and address the king.*

MAG 1   Oh, mighty good one, may you live forever . . .

ENTIRE CAST   And so on and so forth.

MAG 1   We have come up with a response to your question, "What does this mean," that takes in the latest psychological training and human insight.

MAG 2   *[Holding out his hand]* Und der response is . . . Enfelope, please? *[Mag 3 hands him one. He rips it open and all three read:]* WHAT DO *YOU* THINK?

NAR   Strike three. *[As Bel drives magicians away with his bat]* Four, five, six, seven, eight, and nine.

BEL   Now I'll never know what it means.

QUEEN   There, uh, is someone who could tell you.

BEL   *[Brightening]* Really?

QUEEN   He was a magician of your father's. He had the wisdom of the gods. He interpreted dreams and solved crossword puzzles with an ink pen. Your father made him chief of the magicians.

BEL   You don't mean . . .

QUEEN   Oh, yes . . .

BEL   *[Picking up the golden cup and eyeing it nervously]* . . . the little guy who . . .

QUEEN    You got it.

DANIEL    *[Entering]* Hi. I'm Daniel.

BEL    Daniel! I've heard all about you. Look, I know I've ignored you, but if you can solve this riddle, then I'll give you . . .

DANIEL    Sure, sure. I've heard all that stuff. Robes, chains, kingdoms. You can keep it. Purple's not my color. Besides, I don't need that stuff. I'm just here to serve God. *[Taking the cup from Bel]* Who, I see, you think is here to serve you. Where's the writing?

BEL    Over here.

DANIEL    *[Studying it]* "Mene, mene, tekel" and "Parsin."

BEL    Do you know what it means?

DANIEL    Yes. But only because God has told me.

BEL    *[Laughing nervously]* One of my magicians said it was warning that a new season was coming up on network TV!

DANIEL    No, it's worse than that.

BEL    *[Truly horrified]* What can it be!!

DANIEL    Hush up and I'll tell you. Listen: I interpreted dreams for your father. Nice guy. A little arrogant at times, but sooner or later he always humbled himself before God. I liked him

for that. You—you won't humble yourself. You use stuff for your parties that was set apart for God's use, and get drunk with them. You worship weird gods. So God got sick of it, and he wrote this message on the wall.

*He pulls out a pointer and begins to use it.*

DANIEL    "Mene:" God has numbered your days, and the number's come up. "Mene:" God has numbered the days of your kingdom, and it's not in any better shape. "Tekel:" God has weighed you, and you don't cut the mustard. "Parsin:" Ergo, your kingdom's going to be divided and given to the Medes and the Persians.

NAR    What could Belshazzar do? He'd been caught being a jerk about God. So he gave Daniel what he'd promised. Maybe he thought that, if he treated this guy well, God would let him off the hook. But God didn't fall for it, and that very night the enemy came marching in to town and, well . . .

SOLDIER    I'm looking for Belshazzar.

BEL    *[Fearfully]* I'm, uh, him . . .

SOLDIER    Oh, goody!

*He whacks him with a Whiffle® Bat and drags him away.*

NAR    The lesson is simple. Don't fool with God.

*END*

# 12

# DANIEL 6: THE LIONS' DEN

"My God sent his angel, and he shut the mouths of the lions. They have not hurt me, because I was found innocent in his sight" (Dan. 6:22a).

Daniel was gonna pray to *his* God and he didn't care who saw him.

Brave stuff. His wasn't just a case of being laughed at for saying grace in the cafeteria. Getting caught praying could have cost him his life. But for God's intervention, it would have.

It takes courage to stand up for what you believe and Daniel—little more than a teenager—had the wisdom to know the source from which such courage comes: God. And he knew the only way to get that courage was to keep the communication lines open. So he prayed daily, three times. He never said, "Uh, God, it's a little inconvenient right now. People may be watching. I'll catch you after lights out!" He simply got on his knees and prayed, right at the window where he knew people would likely be watching. He didn't pray there to rub his holiness in others' faces, but because he could then look toward his homeland as he offered up petitions for his friends in Jerusalem.

Do we have the courage to pray, no matter who is around? Before an important test, to bless our food, to help us do our best in an oral report or a game? Be a Daniel!

\* \* \*

*Characters:* 7 actors.

NARRATOR

DARIUS
DANIEL
ASHPENAZ
SATRAPS 1 & 2
GUARD

**Props:**
Golf club, two golf balls, empty glass (DARIUS); Whiffle® Bat (GUARD); notepad (ASHPENAZ); magnifying glasses (SATRAPS).

*The set is basically blank, although a lions' den and stepladder will be brought on. The lions' den can be a couple of refrigerator boxes taped together and painted cartoonishly—possibly the flip side of the fiery furnace.*

NAR    Daniel was a prophet who went through an awful lot of hassles. Think about it: taken in his youth from Judah to the kingdom of Nebuchadnezzar he overcame religious persecution to become the greatest of the king's advisors; then he suddenly had to put up with an arrogant heir to the throne, Belshazzar. After Belshazzar bought the farm, he had a whole new king to deal with—Darius was his name.

*Darius, a man in strange golfing clothes and carrying a golf club, comes in. He is followed by Ashpenaz, then by Daniel and satraps 1 & 2 who stand before the king.*

DARIUS   As new king of this nation I plan to keep things in order by setting 120 sandtraps over it.

ASH   That'th thatrapth, thir.

DARIUS   Whatever. Over them I will place you three. We'll see how well you perform.

*All exit.*

NAR   After a time, Darius began to notice something.

*Darius enters with Daniel. He sets a glass on the floor. He begins to practice putting.*

DARIUS   I've begun to notice something, Daniel.

DANIEL   So I've heard.

DARIUS   You've done well. Incredibly well. Fantastically well. Best of all, I can beat you at golf. I'm thinking of placing you over everyone. Would that be alright with you?

DANIEL   Whatever the Lord chooses.

*They exit and satraps enter, sneaking.*

SATRAP 1   Did you hear that? We're going to have to start taking orders from a religious kook.

SATRAP 2   We've got to find some kind of charge to hang Daniel on, or he'll be telling us what to do!

*They whip out magnifying glasses and search the stage, each circling it in an opposite direction.*

NAR   But they couldn't find anything, because Daniel was trustworthy. He wasn't corrupt, and he was a hard worker.

*Satraps finish their circle, bumping forehead to forehead.*

SATRAPS   Nuts.

*Now they sit on their haunches, facing the audience.*

SATRAP 1   There must be something.

SATRAP 2   Somewhere.

SATRAP 1   Somehow.

SATRAP 2   Some way.

SATRAPS   But what?

SATRAP 2   I got it! Through his God!

SATRAP 1   Daniel's God?

SATRAP 2   Who else's? Look, Daniel is big on worshiping only his God.

SATRAP 1   Everyone knows that.

SATRAP 2   Yeah, but King Darius has an ego that won't quit.

SATRAP 1   Stale news!

SATRAP 2   So what if we get King Darius to pass a law requiring everyone to pray to him?

SATRAP 1   And that if anyone prays to anyone else we'll throw them in the lions' den?

SATRAP 2   Darius the god. He'll love it!

SATRAP 1   Daniel the Hebrew. He'll never do it!

SATRAPS   We've got him! *[They exit.]*

NAR   And so their plan was set in motion. Soon Darius made a law requiring everyone in the kingdom to pray to him, and to him alone, to be effective for thirty days.

*Enter satraps.*

SATRAP 1   Let's watch Daniel's house to see what he does!

*They crouch at one corner of the stage. Daniel enters and faces the audience, then kneels.*

SATRAP 2   Look! He's doing it!

NAR   Sure enough, even after hearing about the law, Daniel went to his window three times every day and, facing Jerusalem, he prayed to God.

*Satraps, snickering, exit. Daniel also exits. Darius enters stage left, studying two golf balls, followed by Ashpenaz. Satraps enter stage right.*

SATRAPS   King Darius!

DARIUS   Which do you think is better? The Tru-Flite, or the Marduk Madball?

SATRAP 1   The Marduk, sire. Now, didn't you publish a decree that no one could pray to anyone but you for the next thirty days, and that anyone who did would be thrown to the lions?

DARIUS   Now that's a good question.

ASH   *[Holding up a decree]* It'th right here, thire.

DARIUS   Hmm . . . I guess I did.

SATRAP 2   What's that fine print at the bottom?

DARIUS   *[Reading]* "This decree stands—in accordance with the laws of the Medes and Persians, which cannot be annulled. Hand wash and tumble dry only."

SATRAP 1   Well, Sire, it just so happens that we saw Daniel praying . . .

SATRAP 2   Three times a day!

SATRAP 1   To his Hebrew God. Not you!

SATRAP 2   And he was such a good leader.

SATRAP 1   Guess he'll have to be thrown to the lions.

SATRAP 2   What a shame!

SATRAPS   Tsk! Tsk! Tsk!

DARIUS   *[Horrified]* But not Daniel! He's . . . he's . . . different! He's my friend! I'll never let him go to the lions!

SATRAPS   Remember the fine print!

DARIUS   *[To Ashpenaz]* I'm afraid our friend Daniel has bogeyed on the course.

NAR   What could he do? The lions' den was brought in.

*This is done by one or two guards. The den is a big refrigerator box. Over the lid we see the waving paws of angry lions, and we hear their angry roar. The guard beats them back with the ever-present Whiffle® Bat.*

NAR   And so was Daniel.

*Daniel enters, carrying a stepladder which he sets beside the box. He climbs up.*

DARIUS  I couldn't help it, Daniel! May your God rescue you!

DANIEL  Ciao!

*He jumps in. We hear the lions roar. The satraps snicker and hurry off. Worried, Darius exits as well.*

NAR  Darius really liked Daniel, and he felt pretty stupid for letting his vanity blind him to the satraps' tricks. He didn't sleep well that night, and the next morning everyone rushed back to the lions' den to see what had happened.

*Darius, Ashpenaz, guard(s) and satraps all enter. The satraps climb the ladder and peer in.*

SATRAP 1  I can't wait to see!

SATRAP 2  This is our greatest day!

DANIEL  *[Still out of sight]* Hi, guys.

SATRAP 1  This is not terrifically good news.

SATRAP 2  I didn't know lions could purr.

DARIUS  Daniel! Are you alive!

DANIEL  *[Climbing out of the den]* God sent his angel to protect me! He shut the lions' mouths. They couldn't hurt me because I was innocent in God's sight. And I've never done any wrong to you, Sire!

NAR  The king was overjoyed.
*They hug.*

NAR  And the satraps were kitty food.

*At the guard's command, they jump screaming into the box. We hear the lions roar and see the paws fly as Darius delivers his speech.*

DARIUS  Ashpenaz! Take a letter! "I issue a decree that in every part of my kingdom people must fear and reverence the God of Daniel! For he is the living God who endures for ever and his kingdom will not be destroyed! He has rescued Daniel from the power of the lions!"

ASH  Got it.

DARIUS  You took the letter.

ASH  *[Insulted]* Of courthe.

DARIUS  Read it back to me.

ASH  "Double-you."

DARIUS  AAAARRRRGHH!

*He exits, chasing Ashpenaz with his golf club.*

NAR  And so you see, God protects those who are falsely accused, and will be with them even in the very dens of the lions—if they lean on him.

*END*

# PART THREE

## Taking on the World

# 13

# THE FABLE OF
# THE NEW AGE PIG

"You will not surely die," the serpent said to the woman. "For God knows that when you eat of it . . . you will be like God, knowing good and evil" (Gen. 3:4–5).

Remember Shirley MacLaine in that movie, facing the enormous ocean, looking about as significant as one of the grains of sand she stood on, squealing at the top of her lungs, "I am God!"?

Poor Shirley. She's bought Satan's oldest lie, *You can be like God.* That's what the New Age is all about. You are God. I am God. When you feed your dog tonight, feed him well, because even he is God. New Agers see God as a great pool of energy from which everything is made. The best explanation I've seen of this concept is in the *Star Wars* movies. May the force completely fool you. . . .

As Christians, we all have God in us. But that doesn't make us part of him, or him a literal part of us. It means his Spirit dwells in us and guides us. When Paul speaks of all believers being one body, he doesn't mean we are all part of that same great energy pool named God; he means we are individuals operating as one and united under the leadership of Christ.

No one wants to be bothered with an ultimate Source who sets the rules of right and wrong. The easiest way around this is to deny there is any God (and, therefore, there is no right or wrong) or, better yet, to declare you are one yourself (there is right and wrong, and you are the only legitimate judge of it).

Don't be fooled. Wanting to be God doesn't make you God any more than wanting to be a duck will make you lay eggs.

And that, in a barnyard fable, is what this skit is all about.

\* \* \*

*Characters:*
NARRATOR
SAGE PIG
ENLIGHTENED PIG (E. PIG)
OTHER PIGS
FARMER
FARMER'S WIFE
SPORT (This character is optional)

*For list of props, see index, page 166.*

*While the lines for the Pigs other than the Enlightened Pig (E. Pig) and Sage Pig are numbered as Pig 1, Pig 2, and Pig 3, you can further divide the lines or condense them for any number of the little rooters. Let your pigs walk on two feet—it will be a dramatic mistake to have them squealing about on all fours. Let their mannerisms and a pig nose (even ones made out of plastic foam cups) show that they are pigs.*

NAR   Once upon a time there was a pig farm and it was just full of pigs. They were intelligent pigs who spent a great deal of time wallowing in the mud and manure, and thinking great things about themselves.

*The pigs come out, squealing and oinking.*

NAR   Now, some of these were humble pigs, who had a good deal of respect for the Farmer, a loving and gentle man with no sense of smell, who called the pigs pet names and fed them and cared for them when they were sick.

*The Farmer goes among them, emptying imaginary corn from a pail, sending the pigs into a delighted feeding frenzy.*

NAR   Every night, the pigs who were anxious to learn would gather and listen to the Sage Pig, who spoke deep truths about the Farmer.

*The pigs all gather and the Sage Pig takes his place to speak. The Enlightened Pig also takes a seat, but looks troubled and thoughtful throughout.*

SAGE PIG   For every pig it is appointed once to die, and then the dinner table!

PIG 1   Does the Farmer die?

SAGE PIG   Yes, but he doesn't appear on the dinner plate.

PIG 2   What happens?

SAGE PIG   He goes to something called a judgment. Then he lives in another form, forever.

PIGS   Ooooh!

*The pigs all exit, talking animatedly, leaving the Enlightened Pig who sits, wondering.*

E. PIG   I wish I could avoid the dinner plate.

NAR   Time passed.

E. PIG   It would be wonderful if *I* were the Farmer!

NAR   He sat there all night, thinking.

E. PIG   If *only* I were the Farmer.

NAR   And finally, about daybreak . . .

E. PIG   Hey, *wait* a minute!

NAR   . . . a great revelation hit him . . .

E. PIG   Maybe . . . just *maybe* . . .

NAR   . . . that would change the way pigs thought . . .

E. PIG   . . . not just maybe, but *certainly* . . . !

NAR   . . . for many, many years!

E. PIG   *[Rising and speaking in a loud, thundering piggy voice]* I AM THE FARMER!

*And he stands there, snorting merrily.*

NAR   For the next several days he worked on this theology, carefully watching and imitating the Farmer's every move.

*Enter pigs, stage right. Enter the Farmer, stage left, whistling as he passes the line of pigs. E. Pig leaves the line to follow him, squealing in a terrible imitation of the Farmer's song. The Farmer stops suddenly, turns, and looks at him. They stare at each other, nose to snout, circle one another. The Farmer hurries off, thinking he's got a crazy pig on his hands. E. Pig snorts approvingly.*

NAR    The other pigs were baffled by his strange behavior. But the Enlightened Pig refused to speak to them of his discovery, for he was still figuring it out.

*Farmer enters with his Wife, and they stand among the pigs.*

FARMER    Goin' to town, honey. Kiss me good-bye.

*They kiss. (They may simply turn toward one another, several feet apart, and kiss the air . . . just so the audience realizes this is supposed to be a kiss.) The Farmer leaves. The E. Pig walks up to the wife, puckers up, and she screams, then runs away.*

NAR    Finally, the Enlightened Pig had everything figured out, and he decided to reveal his incredible find to the other pigs.

SAGE PIG    Tonight, I will tell the story of how the Farmer built the barn.

E. PIG    Big whoop.

SAGE PIG    *[Blustering]* What did you say!

E. PIG    I have a great revelation! We are *all* Farmers!

*The pigs titter excitedly.*

SAGE PIG    Nonsense. We are all pigs.

E. PIG    We are pigs, but we have the Farmer in us!

PIGS    What do you mean! Tell us! Tell us!

E. PIG    Don't you see? We think of ourselves as mere pigs only because we are not enlightened! Why, the Farmer is within us! We have only to realize it!

SAGE PIG    This is ridiculous. You're no more the Farmer than I am a duck. The Farmer is not in you. Why, in a little while, *you* shall be in *him!*

E. PIG    But I *am* the Farmer! We all are! We can do anything the Farmer can do, for we *are* the Farmer!

SAGE PIG    Then let's see you build a barn. The Farmer did. Let's see you bring us corn and swill.

NAR    The Sage Pig made sense, but the young pigs chose to overlook this in favor of the Enlightened Pig—for the idea of being farmers pleased them very much.

E. PIG    You see, there is no one single Farmer. The one we see is really just an exalted pig!

PIG 3    An exalted pig!

E. PIG    . . . Who has come to show us the way to the Farmer! The Farmer is a great source made up of us all—we are each a part of the great One Farmer! There's no dinner plate after death! Death is an illusion! Why, you will come back again, and again and again, and if you listen to me and the exalted pig, then you will one day attain near-perfection and come back as exalted pigs, yourselves!

PIG 1    And then?

E. PIG    And then you'll be absorbed into the One Farmer for eternity!

SAGE PIG    *[As the other pigs squeal]* MADNESS! We will never be happy so long as we have this delusion that we are the Farmer! We must accept the fact that we are pigs, cared for by a loving Farmer. Only then can we be happy, for such is our place in life!

E. PIG   You are old fashioned and superstitious. We can never become a truly enlightened society of pigs until your kind is destroyed!

*In fury, the other pigs rise up and attack the Sage Pig, making a terrible noise. They run him away.*

NAR   For the next several days the pigs went about declaring they were farmers, and they were proud. They honored the Farmer when he came, but no more so than the Enlightened Pig, for they knew they could one day come back as exalted pigs, themselves—just as the Farmer had. As for the Enlightened Pig, the others gave him the greatest piles of manure to wallow in, and the best of the corn and swill. He actually got so high-headed that he began to believe he was equal to the Farmer himself.

E. PIG   Well! I'm as exalted as *he* is! I think I'll just go into the farmhouse and sit myself down, and show these other pigs how truly exalted I am!

*Proudly, he trots across the stage to the Farmer's house where the Farmer and the Wife sit at dinner. As he passes his fellow pigs, they squeal excitedly.*

PIG 3   Look! He's going to the exalted pig's house!

PIG 2   How exciting!

PIG 1   This will prove he's really exalted, himself!

*He enters the Farmer's house and plops himself down. The Farmer's Wife screams and runs away. He grins at the Farmer.*

E. PIG   *[Grabbing a mug]* Hello! Snort! Snort! Pour me a hot brew! I've come for dinner!

FARMER   Indeed you have. Just come with me.

*The Farmer leads the E. Pig past the other pigs, who watch in excited amazement. Just before he exits, the Farmer stops long enough to pick up an axe. All watch their exit happily.*

PIG 2   There he goes!

*A loud WHACK! is heard.*

PIG 2   There went a great pig.

PIG 1   Why, we watched one exalted pig and one enlightened pig go around back . . .

PIG 3   But we'll see two exalted pigs return!

NARRATOR   And they waited…

*Farmer walks past, whistling happily.*

PIG 2   That's one!

NAR   . . . all night long.

PIG 3   But where's the other?

PIG 2   These things take time.

NAR   A good deal of time. Finally the next morning, word went around that their great Enlightened Pig was coming out of the house that evening. They gathered excitedly to wait.

*The Farmer walks past carrying a plate full of pork bones.*

FARMER   Here, Sport! Come on, boy! I've got a real treat for you! Come on, boy!

*Sport comes rushing and barking and jumping and yipping. (Or Farmer simply mimes this lunatic dog's presence.) The Farmer scrapes the scraps onto the floor for him and he begins to eat excitedly as the*

78

*Farmer exits, whistling. The pigs watch him gobble up their leader.*

PIG 1    *[After a pause]* He didn't look very exalted to me.

NAR   The moral? If a pig spends all his life believing he's a Farmer, he'll still end up a cooked pig. And so the man who thinks he is a god.

*END*

# 14

# THE PROCEDURE

"Woe to those who call evil good and good evil, who put darkness for light and light for darkness, who put bitter for sweet and sweet for bitter" (Isa. 5:20).

Isaiah was speaking of the idolatrous Hebrews when he said the above, but he might just as well have been speaking about our society today.

The Hebrews watched the practices of their ungodly neighbors and soon bought into their religions, throwing their own children into fires. It was, they reasoned, the proper and unselfish thing to do. Giving up one's child guaranteed the favor of the gods and promised good crops and many cattle. The Hebrews even twisted their own theology as a defense: hadn't Jehovah said the first-born was his? That they would go so far as to advance this ludicrous idea is illustrated when God later told Jeremiah, "I never told them to do that! The thought never entered my mind!" (See Jer. 7:31.)

Today we offer our unborn babies to an abortionist's solvents and suction tubes, sacrificing them to gods of convenience. We rationalize that it is the "loving thing" to do. We have come to the point where covering our own embarrassment and keeping our lifestyle comfortable is more important than a helpless human child's life.

We train our children in the way they will go. I wonder sometimes, what your generation will do—or the generation after you, if abortion is not turned around—as they watch how low a value their parents place on their lives; when they see how unwilling we are to raise them or to at least bring them into the world and place them in the arms of loving adoptive parents.

There's an old saying, "What goes around comes around." When we're old and feeble, an expensive hindrance to our children's lives, will they remember how we treated the unwanted members of *their* generation? And will they "lovingly" euthanize us?

* * *

*Characters:*
   DOCTOR
   YOUNG WOMAN
   OLD MAN

*For list of props, see index, page 166.*

*An office. The Doctor paces about, talking, while the woman sits and—mostly—reacts to the words that are spoken. He is confident, professional, friendly but not warm. She is insecure, frightened, feeling trapped by her unfortunate "circumstance." The Doctor, of course, has only the best things in mind. He refers occasionally to a notepad or chart.*

DOCTOR   Well. We've talked of your unfortunate... *social* situation, haven't we? And you've spoken with Ann, at the clinic? Very good. I recommended her for the position myself. She feels you should undergo the procedure, and I agree with her conclusion.

WOMAN   I'm not so sure . . .

DOCTOR   It's painless, I assure you. Modern technology has made the procedure ridiculously easy. A quick injection, and before you know it, it's done.

WOMAN   I don't know . . . I'm so confused.

DOCTOR   I realize that. I don't like to say it, but you made a serious mistake when you went to that so-called support organization. You should have known it was nothing more than a front for the pro-life movement. Their tactics are so . . . underhanded. They should be outlawed! But, don't worry. We're working to end their influence.

WOMAN   But . . . they told me that . . .

DOCTOR   I know what they told you. Don't ask me the questions, I already know them. I'll ask them for you.

Isn't it murder? No. Murder, you see, is the illegal taking of a life for an unjust reason. The Supreme Court has left no questions as to the legality of the procedure.

Isn't it morally wrong? What is "moral?" What is "immoral?" "Immoral" is any group denying you the right to live your life as you see fit, without being weighed down and inconvenienced by this thing.

*She reacts to the word, "thing."*

DOCTOR   Ah! They've grilled that "It's-not-a-thing-it's-a-human-being" point into you, have they?

WOMAN   I live with this every day. I know he has life.

DOCTOR   *[A caustic echo]* He!

WOMAN   He reacts to things I do!

DOCTOR   Many flowers open in the morning and close at night—they're reacting . . . to the sun. But that doesn't mean they have self-realization. "He" as you call it is living tissue, yes. But nothing more. You've been in this—this predicament—for months. Has "he" spoken to you? Reacted in any way that shows self-realization? No? I thought not.

I can take care of "him." Come now: you carry minimal insurance. You're unmarried. You work full-time at a low-paying job. And you don't have the support of your family. Even if you get financial help, do you realize what you're letting yourself in for? Every free moment you have will be devoured! You'll never be able to enjoy things again. You'll spend every minute spoon-feeding and cleaning up messes. You'll be enslaved, never able to better yourself! You'll never carry out your dreams! How can you let anything be so selfish as to deny you your right to life?

WOMAN   But aren't I denying *him* . . . ?

DOCTOR   *[Another sarcastic echo]* Him! If I have a cancerous growth removed, have I denied *it?* Of course not. Be sensible. You didn't want this. No one does. Show true love: go through the procedure. Terminate this tissue! It's the only logical thing for your situation! Will you?

*A pause. Slowly, she nods "yes."*

DOCTOR   Good. It's the wise choice. I'll leave now, and we'll bring the injection in just a few minutes. Meantime, you get things ready.

*He gives her a friendly clap on the shoulder and leaves. She sits a moment, confused, crying. Then she rises, exits, and comes back, leading a very sick, senile old man. He is bent, confused, trembling as he looks about, wide-eyed. Somehow we can't help but feel he knows, even through his fog of confusion, that something terrible is about to take place.*

WOMAN   Come, Grandpa. You sit here and wait. You stay here, and be good, and someone will be along any minute. They'll give you something that'll make everything better. For both of us.  Oh God!

*She hugs him and runs away. He stares about.*

*END*

# 15

# NOT JUST BLACK AND WHITE

"Rescue those being led away to death; hold back those staggering toward slaughter. If you say, 'But we knew nothing about this,' does not he who weighs the heart perceive it? . . . Will he not repay each person according to what he has done?" (Prov. 24:11–12a).

You've heard all the arguments favoring legalized abortion. We can't really prove when life begins (so why are we taking chances?). If we outlaw abortions, people will have them anyway (so let's legalize burglary!). Unwanted children will be born (the couples awaiting adoption exceeds the number of abortions performed). No one would adopt a handicapped child (the waiting lists are very long for handicapped children such as those afflicted with spina bifida).

The arguments are packed with holes and mortared with faulty logic. We call an unborn child a "baby" when we want it and television news crews stand in wondrous awe over surgery which "saves the unborn child's life!" But if the baby is unwanted, the media and abortion advocates suddenly start calling it a "fetus" and even "fetal tissue."

Today we watch as people blocking abortion clinics are arrested and sentenced with heavy fines and long jail terms. We refuse to picket or counsel, to write our legislators, to discuss the issue with friends, or even to sign petitions. We run for cover when we hear the media's cry of "women's rights," when we should be responding with, "what about the rights of these children?" What will God say to *us* on the last day?

Do you remember the holocaust? Good citizens and Christians went about privately stating they were, personally, opposed to mistreatment of the Jews, but they refused to take steps to change Hitler's policy. Many refused to speak against it. Only a handful were willing to actively stand up for what was right, willing to pay the consequences of unpopularity, arrest, and even terms in Nazi death camps. The result? Millions of Jews and other "undesirables" were butchered in the name of the fatherland.

Perform this skit and see if the similarities between the two aren't uncanny.

*This is a series of vignettes involving a number of characters. The actors may double up on parts, using simple costume and prop changes to identify new characters. The stage should be simple—chairs, benches, possibly a small desk. Keep costumes in shades of gray, black, and white. Use very little color.*

*As players in one vignette walk offstage, players for the next one walk on. The effect should be fluid, very strong, never giving the audience a moment to breathe.*

*For list of props, see index, page 166.*

\* \* \*

*Characters:* 6-13 actors (many parts can double) as follows:

SCENE TWO:
BAKER

SCENE THREE:
MOMMA
POPPA
HANS
GRETA

SCENE FOUR:
OFFICER
JEW
CONSTABLE
AGENT

SCENE FIVE:
MAYOR
SECRETARY

SCENE SIX:
ALICE
JILL

## SCENE ONE

*The Opening*

*Actors enter and march to an area upstage where a portrait of Hitler hangs behind a desk, possibly with a Nazi flag to one side. They salute the portrait, shouting, "Seig Heil!" Actors then leave the stage and stand off to either side of it, motionless.*

## SCENE TWO

*The Baker*

*The Baker enters, carrying a loaf of bread. He is a friendly, though guilt-ridden, man.*

BAKER   I am a good man, an ethical man, a Christian! And when I see how this madman Hitler treats the Jews in the fatherland—and in the countries he has annexed—I am sick. Physically sick.

After all, they are people, the Jews. Industrious and loving, as valuable and as important as anyone else. They are innocent of any wrong-doing! And when I see people kick them and club them down in the streets, when I watch as they are loaded onto the trains and buses that take them off to be gassed, I say to myself: this is an atrocity! We must find a better solution!

So you see? We agree, you and I. And yet, it isn't just black and white, as many of these pastors and churchmen are claiming.

We have to face the fact that their presence does cause a problem across the fatherland. Through no fault of their own, surely: it is the people who refuse to accept them—who refuse to help them or give them a decent place in society. And yet, simply telling our people that we can no longer kill Jews will not end the problem of what to do with the unwanted Jews.

Deporting human beings to prison camps to be gassed! A horrible death. Horrible! But to outlaw it and allow all these people in a land where they are unwanted is not right, either. You are right, we must find a moral solution for these Jews. But until we come up with one, until such a plan exists and is ready to run, what else can be done? We must be patient. We must let this gassing of Jews continue until we have a better way.

*He exits.*

## SCENE THREE

*The Family*

*The Family—Momma, Poppa, Hans, and Greta— gather around the table. They bow as though praying. Momma is strong and domineering; Poppa is meek, soft-spoken.*

HANS    . . . And God bless Momma, and Poppa, Mr. Rubenstein *[Momma and Poppa glance at one another]*, and dinner too!

GRETA    Silly! You pray for dinner like you pray for bed!

HANS    I do not!

POPPA    *[Tucking his napkin in]* At least he didn't bless the whole schoolyard this time, or dinner would be cold!

*All laugh, and the children also tuck in their napkins—just like Poppa.*

MOMMA    Why did you bless Mr. Rubenstein?

HANS    He's a funny man! He wears that funny star!

GRETA    I like him.

HANS    Me too! I'm glad he lives upstairs.

POPPA    He is a pleasant man, and smart, too. *[He taps his head to indicate this.]*

HANS & GRETA    *[Imitating him]* Yes! Very smart!

GRETA    Why does he wear the star?

MOMMA    He is a Jew.

HANS    Our teacher says he killed Jesus. *[Parents react with consternation.]*

POPPA    Of course he didn't!

MOMMA    Jesus died thousands of years ago!

HANS    Our teacher said his people did it, and God blames all of them, even now.

GRETA    That includes Mr. Rubenstein.

HANS    They make fun of us at school because we like him.

GRETA    They say we support Jesus killers, and that makes us guilty too.

POPPA    What do you say to them?

HANS    I tell them my Poppa would never kill Jesus, and I'll wallop anyone who says otherwise!

GRETA    I heard Fraü Hunt talking after school and she said you're both enemies of the state because you let Mr. Rubenstein come to dinner, and Fraü Grotten says you probably help Mr. Rubenstein sacrifice children.

*Poppa and Momma are panicked at this.*

HANS    I'll wallop her good!

POPPA    Of course you won't!

MOMMA    Go play now, both of you.

*The children exit.*

MOMMA    Enemies of the state! Our neighbors think we're not patriotic, that we don't love the fatherland! We've got to do something.

POPPA    Mr. Rubenstein is a very nice man.

MOMMA    *They* say the Jews are causing problems everywhere!

POPPA    That's propaganda. You know that.

MOMMA    What does it matter? It's making us lose our friends! We are a laughingstock! Look what it's doing to Hans and Greta! We could lose our lives!

POPPA    What do you want me to do? Turn him in to the Gestapo?

MOMMA    Yes! Yes! That would do it. We'd save face if he were gone.

POPPA    But that would be wrong! He's done nothing other than be a Jew!

MOMMA    Of course it's wrong, but it's not just black and white like that. By knowing him, by having him in our house, we are humiliated! "Jesus killers"! They're calling us Jesus killers, and we're good Christian people. I am going to call the Gestapo and tell them where they can find him, at his shop. And you will not stop me!

POPPA    Whatever you want, Momma.

MOMMA    It is for a greater good! It is for our well-being!

*She exits. Poppa sits. He knows it is wrong but cannot bring himself to stop her. He lifts a cup to drink—but he only brings it halfway before he stops. He stares vacantly ahead.*

POPPA    Now. Now we are Jesus killers. *[He shakes his head.]*

## SCENE FOUR

*The Depot*

*The Officer, the Jew (in handcuffs), and the Constable enter and sit at a bench. Constable glances at her watch.*

CONSTABLE    Where is he?

OFFICER    He will come.

CONSTABLE    He's late.

OFFICER    You have another minute. He is always on time.

CONSTABLE    This is distasteful. I want to get it over with.

*Officer laughs, glances at the Jew.*

OFFICER    *This* is distasteful!

*He opens a book (perhaps* Mein Kampf) *and begins to read. Agent enters from opposite side of the stage—this is a precise, cold person in a suit, wearing Nazi armbands.*

AGENT    Fraülein Deitrich?

CONSTABLE    Herr Hoffman?

AGENT    This is the Jew?

CONSTABLE    It is.

AGENT    *[To Officer]* Take her to the car. We will drive her to headquarters where she can join the others.

*Officer pulls the Jew to her feet and walks off with her. Constable watches them leave, rubbing her hands guiltily.*

AGENT  *[Smiling knowingly]* A good hand-cream would take care of that dry skin, Fraülein.

CONSTABLE  Thank you, Herr Hoffman.

AGENT  You do not enjoy this. You do not approve of our "solution."

CONSTABLE  *[Quietly]* I think it's wrong. But I know it's just not as simple as that. It's not all black and white.

AGENT  So why did you do it?

CONSTABLE  The people of this city did not want her around. They have grown hostile toward her kind, and they have thrown stones at her. Soon she will not be allowed to buy bread, and life will become very bad for her. I thought it would be kinder to send for you and just have it over with.

AGENT  To spare her suffering later on?

CONSTABLE  Taking her now is more humane, isn't it?

AGENT  You have made the right choice. The right to have a choice is why we do this with these . . . Jews.

CONSTABLE  It's quick, isn't it? She won't suffer.

AGENT  What do you think? Heil Hitler!

CONSTABLE  *[Meekly]* Heil Hitler.

*He exits left. She exits right.*

## SCENE FIVE

*The Mayor's Office*

*The Mayor enters and sits at the desk. His secretary enters behind him and sets a paper before him. She stands back as he dips a fountain pen into a bottle and prepares to write.*

SECRETARY  *[Sarcastic]* So Herr Mayor, so pious and mighty! You are going to sign it, are you?

MAYOR  *[Equally snide]* Yes, Fraü Secretary, that is what I have the pen for. The council approved my bill. Now I shall sign it into law.

SECRETARY  They approved it only because you bullied them into it. Now the entire city must follow *your* sense of right and wrong! Regardless of the fact the entire fatherland sees it another way!

MAYOR  The "entire" fatherland does not. It is just a small but vocal minority who is duping us all into thinking that abusing the Jews is right.

SECRETARY  And I am one of the duped?

MAYOR  I never said that. Besides, the council . . .

SECRETARY  . . . has the backbone of a slug! You got onto your platform and banged your fist and shouted self-righteous nonsense and bullied them into something they know can never work!

MAYOR  Now listen. This bill to protect the Jews of this city is important and right.

SECRETARY  It is *your* morality that says it is right. Many of us believe they are a great problem to our society. You are forcing *your* morals on us, and that is wrong. Be sensible! Throw this bill away.

MAYOR   How can I! When I see these people being lynched by mobs . . . ! It is wrong!

SECRETARY   Look. I agree with you. Personally, I think it is wrong, too. But it's not just black and white, like that. There are many people who believe the Jewish problem is real, and that they should be eliminated. They believe it sincerely, they have been taught this by Hitler's propaganda machine. If you sign this into law, you will be making criminals of people who sincerely believe they are doing right. Will you arrest people for exercising a right they believe they should have?

MAYOR   I'm not saying they're criminals for killing the Jews . . . just misled. It is the leaders of these mobs who will be arrested.

SECRETARY   And you think that will stop them? The old Jew who was hung last night? They believed they were doing something patriotic. If you make it against the law, they will still do it. They will still lynch them. They will still deport them. Give it up. Why make criminals of honest people? Don't sign the thing, throw it in the trash! We will burn it in the square tonight with all the books, eh?

*He looks slightly perplexed. She exits. He smiles, nods that she was correct, wads up the bill, and throws it away.*

## SCENE SIX

*A Restaurant*

*Back to America: we hear a modern song on the radio, and a DJ saying, "Light rock of the 90s, thanks for making the switch to WDVI." Jill and Alice sit having a Coke. As they talk they grow more upset with one another.*

ALICE   Look, Jill, I agree that abortion is wrong.

JILL   Why do you believe it? Because it's the taking of an innocent human life, right?

ALICE   Well, yeah, sure. But it isn't like you're making it sound. I mean, what do we do about the unwanted crack babies? What about homes where the babies won't be loved or they might be abused? What about rape and incest, where the woman has to live with that reminder of the terrible experience for nine months?

JILL   Listen. You agreed that a fetus is an innocent human life.

ALICE   Yes, but it's not just black and white like that! What about . . .

JILL   Wait. Try this: Imagine Nazi Germany. Try your argument out, using the word "Jew" instead of "fetus." *Then* tell me it's not just black and white.

*She gets up and walks off. Alice sits a moment, throws up her arms in disgust, and gets up to follow. She stops suddenly, letting Jill's suggestion sink in a little, then exits.*

*END*

# PART FOUR

## All About God and Christians

# 16

# JUDGMENT JEOPARDY

"You believe that there is one God. Good! Even the demons believe that—and shudder" (James 2:19).

Jesus was sending a message for John to deliver to the church at Laodicea. "Tell those people I know all about their deeds," he said. "Tell them they're not hot, and they're not even cold. I wish they were one or the other, because I can't stand lukewarm Christians. If they don't shape up, I'll spit them out of my mouth!"

I can think of no more greatly wasted lives than those people who pretend they follow Jesus, but don't really know him or love him at all. Why do they bother? They're bringing condemnation on themselves, earning the disgust of the world, and ruining the Christian witness while they're at it.

A relationship with God must be total. Going through the motions is meaningless as far as our Lord is concerned. Sometimes, by doing that, we can fool other Christians and even get their admiration. But nobody fools God. Sooner or later, come judgment day, all those hypocrites' loved ones will see what frauds they were.

It's a lesson to remember. Too bad poor Fred Smarm didn't learn it before he found himself being a contestant on Judgment Jeopardy.

*This skit will work best with all the sound effects: bells, buzzers, horns. If you can concoct a Jeopardy board with sliding or turning panels, that'll add to the effect, too. But you can also manage by having the Emcee refer to an imaginary board just offstage. Do try to get the buzzers in, though. Those little gadgets with laser beams, bombs, machine guns, and other sound effects that you can buy for frustrated drivers work well.*

\* \* \*

*Characters:*
   GABE, THE EMCEE
   THE CONTESTANTS:
   #1, GEORGE HEAD, an acid
      rocker and party freak
   #2, ALICE DINGY, a chronic
      social drinker
   #3, FRED SMARM, a seemingly godly man
   A COUPLE OF GUARDS, dressed in
      black
   WINDOW TURNER (if a board is
      used)

*For list of props, see index, page 166.*

*At start: the three contestants' podiums and a Jeopardy board. On the board we see nine panels placed in three rows of three panels each, hiding answers. At the top of each row is an identifying sign: BIBLE VERSES, PEOPLE WHO KNOW JESUS, and PEOPLE WHO DON'T KNOW JESUS. Everyone is chipper at the start of the game, although the contestants become continuously more nervous as the time goes by. Gabe, however, is cheery and all smiles right to the very end.*

*Each makes entrance as follows: Gabe and the window turner enter first and take their places. Then the guards enter from the aisle, leading the contestants. Guards play the television Jeopardy theme on kazoos. The contestants take their places at their podiums, and the guards exit.*

*Gabe is wearing an all-white suit. He waves to the audience.*

GABE   Hi, everybody, I'm Mr. Gabe, your host on Judgment Jeopardy, the show where we give you the answer, and *you* come up with the question! Let's meet our contestants for the day. Our first is George Head, all the way from Wilkes-Barre, Pennsylvania! Tell us something about yourself, George!

GEORGE   Like, man, hey, I'm really into heavy metal, crack, casual love, and partying, man.

GABE   And Contestant Number Two is Alice Dingy.

ALICE   Hi, Gabe. I just love hitting the sauce.

GABE   The old demon rum, eh?

ALICE   Oh, yes, and I've got the jolly red nose to prove it!

*Polite laughter.*

GABE   Yes, it's really cute with all those broken blood vessels there. And finally our last contestant, an active man in his community, a real success who is a deacon in his church, Fred Smarm. Fred?

FRED   [Looking around in a daze] Somehow, I thought Judgment Day would be so different.

GABE   That's how it goes on Judgment Jeopardy! We have three categories today. Bible Verses,

People Who Know Jesus, and People Who Don't Know Jesus! We'll let George begin this round.

GEORGE   I'll take Bible Verses for a hundred, man.

GABE   The answer is "For God so loved the world."

FRED   "What is John 3:16," Gabe! I'll take Bible Verses for 200.

GABE   The answer is "First Chronicles 4:3."

ALICE   "What is, 'Take a little wine for the stomach's sake!'"

GABE   I'm sorry, that's the wrong verse.

ALICE   You mean there's other verses?

GABE   You never memorized any others?

ALICE   I never wanted to quote any others.

FRED   I know the question, Gabe! "What is the reference for 'These were the sons of Etam: Jezreel, Ishma and Idbash; and the name of their sister was Hazzelelponi'?"

GABE   You seem to know them all, Fred!

FRED   I really study the Word, Gabe. I'll finish off Bible Verses for 300.

GABE   The answer is, "The love chapter."

GEORGE   Like, wow, that's out of the Stone Age, man. What is "She loves me, Yeah Yeah Yeah?"

GABE   No, no, no, George.

FRED   The question is "What is 1 Corinthians 13!"

GABE   That's right. Fred is ahead, 600 to nothing to zip.

FRED   I'll try People Who Know Jesus for 100.

GABE   "Blind Bartimaeus."

GEORGE   Like, I know that! Like, "Who is the opening act for Twisted Sister?"

GABE   [Painfully] Wrong! Fred.

FRED   "Who was a man that Jesus healed," Gabe! I'll take People Who Know Jesus for 200!

GABE   The answer is, "He danced when he was filled with the Spirit."

*Alice rings in. Knowing what's coming and, thus, burying his face in his hands, Gabe acknowledges her.*

GABE   Alice . . . ?

ALICE   [Excited at knowing one] "Who is Jim Beam?"

GABE   Oh, Alice! How about you, Fred?

FRED   "What did King David do?"

GABE   Yes! And you hold the lead with 900 points.

FRED   I'll finish with People Who Know Jesus for 300!

*Bleeps, gongs, and bells.*

GABE   Oh! A Daily Double! And as you know in Judgment Jeopardy, *anyone* is eligible to give the question. The answer is, "Arnold Hoffmanster."

GEORGE   Hey! Like, "What's my neighbor doing up there?"

GABE   The answer should have been, "Who is my neighbor?" But, judges? Yes! We'll let you have it.

GEORGE   Like, I know him! I used to jam with him till he got religion, man. Then I couldn't stand all his Jesus talk, like, you know? He didn't like cruisin' the babes, an' he started readin' that Bible. Then he told me to get Jesus, man, and I, like, you know, told him where he could go.

GABE   Funny you should say that, George, because that's just what I'm going to tell you. You've got 600 points, but it won't do you any good. You refused Jesus and that's all it takes to lose Judgment Jeopardy.

*Guards come out and drag him, screaming, away.*

ALICE   Boy, I didn't know the stakes would be this high.

FRED   What will the sponsor say?

GABE   "Well done, good and faithful servant," if you win, Fred. By forfeit, the next answer is chosen by Alice.

ALICE   I guess it'll have to be People Who Don't Know Jesus for 100.

GABE   The answer is "Belshazzar."

ALICE   [Nervously] "What is the real name of Spuds McKenzie?"

GABE   So sorry!

FRED    [*No longer so sure of himself*] "Who was the king who saw the handwriting on the wall?"

GABE    That's right! You're up to 1,000 points.

FRED    I'll, uh, take People Who Don't Know Jesus for 200.

GABE    The answer is, "Caiaphas."

ALICE    Wait a minute! "He knew Jesus!" I remember that from Sunday school!

GABE    Yes, but he only knew him as a common man and teacher, no better than anyone else.

ALICE    Well, isn't that who he was?

*Buzzer.*

GABE    I'm sorry, Alice! *Real* sorry! But if you *really* know Christ, you'd know he is God Incarnate and King of Kings! That means, you lose.

*Guards come out and drag her, screaming, away.*

FRED    [*Tugging nervously at his collar*] Uh . . . the question is, "Who was the high priest who called for Jesus' death?"

GABE    And that brings you to 1,200 points, Fred! There's one last window under People Who Don't Know Jesus, and the answer is . . .

FRED    Wait a minute!

GABE    What's wrong, Fred?

FRED    What if . . . I mean . . . I'm not sure I want to see the next answer.

GABE    We can't end the game until we do, Fred.

FRED    But what if it's . . . ?

GABE    Yes?

FRED    Oh, nothing. I read my Bible, don't I?

GABE    You certainly do!

FRED    And I give to the church, right?

GABE    Can't deny it!

FRED    Okay! Go for it!

GABE    The answer is, "FRED SMARM!"

FRED    Oh my heavens! That can't be me!

GABE    Question the answer, Fred.

FRED    "That can't be me, can it? It can be another Fred, right?"

*Buzzer.*

GABE    No, the answer should be, "That must be me, right? No one else would have such a dorky name, right?"

FRED    But *I know Jesus!*

GABE    Fred, Fred. The board doesn't lie. Too bad you do.

FRED    I know my Bible through and through!

GABE    So did Jim Jones, Fred! So did Caiaphas!

FRED    But I give to the church! I attend regularly! I'm on the board! I make my kids do devotions!

GABE    Yes, but you also bilked your insurance company of thousands of dollars by faking an injury!

FRED  They'll never miss it.

GABE  You cheat on your taxes!

FRED  Everyone does!

GABE  You tell the dirtiest jokes the world has known!

FRED  I just want to fit in with my co-workers!

GABE  You never pray at business lunches.

FRED  My clients would think I was nuts!

GABE  And you had an affair with that lovely young Jeneane Hubba!

FRED  I did not!

GABE  Doing it in thought's the same as doing it in fact, Fred! You know that, it's in the book!

FRED  But . . . !

GABE  In fact, she was the Daily Double answer for People Who Know Jesus, yesterday! Well, Fred, you know what this means . . .

FRED  But I've got 1200 points!

*Guards come out and drag him, screaming, away.*

GABE  That's it for today's Judgment Jeopardy. Join us tomorrow for a biggie, when the contestants are Herman Shmilk, Arlene Mungox, and Adolph Hitler! I'm Mr. Gabe, and remember, it's not that you know *of* him that counts, but that you *know* him!

*END*

# 17

# RESTAURANT CHRISTIANS

"A man is not a Jew if he is only one outwardly, nor is circumcision merely outward and physical. No, a man is a Jew if he is one inwardly; and circumcision is circumcision of the heart, by the Spirit, not by the written code. Such a man's praise is not from men, but from God" (Rom. 2:28–29).

Mankind is so caught up with rules and images! You aren't cool unless you *look* cool. Some of the most shallow people are those who go so far out of their way to maintain an "image." The same holds true in church circles; no one thinks you're Christian unless you look Christian.

Paul freaked out pretty regularly over the legalistic Christians who insisted everyone had to follow all the Old Testament laws of circumcision, diet, and cleanliness to be true believers. These people, Paul insisted, were overlooking the important matters of the *heart* in following Jesus.

Jesus himself put across the same idea when he told the Pharisees they were "whitewashed tombs . . . beautiful on the outside but . . . full of dead men's bones" (Matt. 23:27).

Real Christians must wear business suits. Real Christians don't eat meat—they're vegetarians! Real Christians are Republicans, don't listen to—*gasp!*—Christian rock, and do say "Praise the Lord!" at least once every other hour. Real Christians, of course, never, ever go to the movies. That's legalism.

But there's another extreme. Some people believe that, if you're going to encourage others to become Christian, you must look and act so much like the world that there's virtually no difference between you or anyone else.

Don't buy into such garbage. Read your Bible and seriously listen to (and then prayerfully think through) the things your leaders teach at church.

Don't be an image follower. Be a Jesus follower.

* * *

*Characters*:
CONFUSED
EXPLAINER

*Okay. We didn't name the characters in this skit and there's a reason. The characters should go by the names of the actors who play them. They can be both men, both women, or one man and one woman.*

*Everything should be a product of the actors' imaginations: the customers, the menus, the food—even the waitress, Miss Wappleton. Remember, if the actors use their imaginations well, the audience will too.*

*This is a skit that will lend well to ad-libbed lines. If you've got a couple of particularly outgoing kids who work well together, let them feel free to rephrase and add their own thoughts and mannerisms—this will give the skit extra vitality and realism. For a particularly off-the-wall street witness you might try taking this into a real restaurant and springing it on some unwary noontime customers. Make sure the manager knows it's about to happen, of course.*

*At start: a table with chairs. The setting is a restaurant. You might go ahead and use actual menus, a restaurant-style sugar container, water glasses, whatever. But keep most other things in the imagination. Dress is casual. The two enter and go to their table. They are apparently good friends.*

CON   Come on, I don't believe you.

EXP   But it's true!

CON   You cannot tell Christians from anyone else just by looking at them!

EXP   I'm tellin' ya, you can do it—sincere ones and otherwise—at a glance!

CON   Okay. How?

EXP   You just have to be an expert like me.

CON   Expert what?

EXP   Expert Christian hunter.

CON   Oh, come on!

EXP   Sure! Using the tricks and secrets of a Christian hunter, you can find Christians anywhere. Let me show you how. Just pick somebody out, and I'll tell you all about them.

CON   Who?

EXP   Anyone! Any customer in this restaurant.

CON   Okay. How about those three guys over there?

EXP   You mean those guys in the dark suits, the narrow ties, the white shirts?

CON   Yeah. Those old geeky-looking guys.

EXP   *[After considering]* No. I don't think so. But you see those three guys? Over there?

CON   You mean the guys in the dark suits, the narrow ties, the white shirts?

EXP   Yeah! The geeky ones! Now *they're* Christians, beyond a doubt.

CON   But they look just like those other guys, and you said *they* weren't! How can you tell the difference?

EXP   Well, that's Christian Hunter's Secret Number One: It's a case of the face.

CON   Come again?

EXP   The face tells everything! Look at those guys.

      *[He makes an awful, pinched-up face]*

You can tell they haven't smiled since the day they were born again!

CON   *[Laughing]* I see what you mean! It's that easy, huh? Just their expressions?

EXP   Well, Christian Hunters never disregard the clothing, either. That's just as important. It all is: how people look, how they dress, how they act—it all comes together not just to show if you've found a Christian, but what kind of Christian you've got. There are different kinds, you know.

CON   Yeah, well, there's sincere ones and sort-of-sincere ones.

EXP   *[Illustrating as he/she speaks]* Praise-the-Lord! ones and I-guess-I-am ones!

CON   [Getting into it] MY WAY! Christians and, of course, the Hey-God-is-love-so-anything's-cool ones. So what are these guys?

EXP   [He studies a moment] Clothes say Presbyterians. Faces say . . . board of trustees.

*A "waitress" appears. She is not an actress, but a figment of the actors' imaginations.*

EXP   Oh! Hi! I'll have a Coke, a Billy Boy Burger, and a side of fries. How about you?

CON   I'll have the same.

EXP   [To waitress] That's all. What? Looking at? Us? Nothing! Who? Them?

CON   We . . . we were just staring off into space.

EXP   Whose space? Uh . . . [Indicating their subjects] Their space. Alright, we were looking at them. It's just that . . . well, see that guy? Something was hanging from his nose.

CON   [Nodding] That's right! His nose. *What* was hanging from his nose?

*They look at each other.*

CON   A bat!

EXP   A bat?

BOTH   Yes! A bat!

CON   [Aside] She doesn't believe us.

EXP   [To waitress] It was a joke! Ha! Ha! Yes, I suppose that Johnny Carson could have delivered it better. . . . Well, that'll be all, Miss . . . Miss . . . Wappleton. [Apparently she exits.] Strange lady.

CON   Where were we?

EXP   Christian hunting.

CON   Of course.

EXP   Oh! See that guy over there? Thin on top, thick on middle? Wearing the violent canary yellow suit?

CON   Uh-huh.

EXP   I've seen him here before. Last time he came, his suit was so bright it set off the sprinkler system. He has 30 pairs of shoes . . . all white. Except for the brown ones with the pennies in them . . . he uses those for funerals. Any guesses?

CON   You just know he's got to be a preacher. Either Baptist, Methodist, or Independent.

EXP   You're catching on! Let's try a couple more while we're waiting for our order. How about those two groups; the one at the table, and the one waiting to be seated?

CON   Okay. The ones at the table look pretty average. Average hairstyles, average clothes . . . nice, but not fancy, you know? They just seem to be out for a little fun. The way they're laughing and talking, I'd guess they've found it.

EXP   Yeah. Shame they're not Christians. But check out that other group. Ratty jeans, hairstyles by Lawn Boy. And that T-shirt that says "I'm 3rd"? Gives it away, huh? They're either from the local community theater group, college students, or maybe both.

CON   How can you be so sure about them?

EXP   Christian hunting can be easy because so many Christians make their witness through their clothes. For instance, our bored trustees want the rest of the world to know that they're above "those sinful creatures." And our actors are desperate to let the world know that "Christians aren't no different than nobody else, hyuck! hyuck!" They don't want to put on airs.

CON    So instead they put on . . . *that.*

EXP    Exactly.

CON    But not all Christians are like that! Some just like to look their best, and they happen to believe that morticians carry the beacon of fashion in America. And other Christians are just more comfortable wearing ratty jeans.

EXP    The difference is, *they* let their faith be their witness, and Christ is their raiment. Their clothes are just . . . decoration. But our friends here, I fear, are in some danger of, well . . .

CON    . . . letting their clothes and attitudes become their raiment... and Jesus their decoration.

EXP    Exactly.

CON    But isn't it possible that some Christians might have escaped our notice on the grounds of appearing normal?

EXP    Well, sure. But we've got one last, foolproof trick to try!

CON    Namely?

EXP    What's any good Christian going to do when he gets his meal?

CON    He's going to pray!

EXP    You're quick! Now look around. See the guy in the yellow suit? He got his order ten minutes ago and he's still praying over it.

CON    Definitely a preacher! And that "normal" group—they're holding hands and one is leading in a quiet prayer.

EXP    Okay. So I was wrong. They're Christians!

CON    *[Looking about]* Those must be the only Christians! They're the only ones praying.

EXP    Aha! Your amateurism is showing through. You see, you're looking for the wrong kind of prayer! There are different kinds, you know.

CON    Like the holding hands prayer, the folding hands prayer?

EXP    Right! And at the restaurant you have . . .

*Experienced pretends to receive his/her order, looks worriedly about, then briefly bows his/her head and rubs the forehead as if in pain.*

CON    . . . The headache prayer!

EXP    Exactly! The headache prayer is the Christian's compromise to not compromise with God. In it, he manages to make it both look like he's praying and camouflage the fact that he is at the same time! That way you can't really accuse him of not praying, and you can't really prove that he is.

CON    So, if he's fast enough, he gets a blessing. If he isn't, he'll get two aspirin from the waitress.

EXP    You've got it. And I call it the headache prayer because, while *he* sits there pretending to have a headache for God above, God above is . . .

CON   Oh! Here's our order! Thank you, Miss Wappleton, and may God bless you! *[Apparently, "Miss Wappleton" replies . . . ]* Yes, and may God help us.

*They turn to their food, and apparently are not thrilled at the sight before them.*

EXP   "So! How did you find your hamburger, sir?"

CON   "Oh, I just moved the pickle and there it was!"

EXP   Is it alive, or is it Memorex? Well? Shall we pray?

CON   Let's!

*They both bow their heads.*

EXP   Lord, bless this food . . .

*They both grin and, at the same moment, rub their foreheads and grimace as if in pain.*

BOTH   Ow! Ow! Ow!

*Laughing, they both take a bite of their "sandwiches."*

*END*

# 18

# THE EDUCATION INTERVIEW

"In everything set them an example by doing what is good" (Titus 2:7a).

A basic rule of theater is that action speaks louder than words. One actor can be delivering a moving and beautiful speech while every teary eye is glued to him. But let just one player in the back stumble over a pot and do a pratfall, and everyone turns from the competent speaker to gawk at the klutz.

The same idea works in real life. You can speak nobly and tell the world what a fine, upstanding person you are. But if you aren't living that life then all those who are close to you—and someday that will include your children—will know better. And, because you don't live what you teach, they'll be turned off to your ideas.

Proverbs tells us to train our children in the way they should go. Then, when they grow up, even if they stray for a while they'll eventually come back to the life they were taught. And by teaching we don't mean the way their parents talked, but how they *lived*.

Your parents send you to youth group because they know it is best for you, even though there are nights when you'd rather be doing something else. Some parents, however, let their children stay away from church whenever they want, rather than argue. They say that Christianity is the most important thing in their lives—but their kids aren't fooled.

Remember this when you have your own children. If you don't think church is important enough to make them take part in it (and if you don't do so yourself), then they'll grow up thinking it's an unimportant part of life. And remember the next time your parents make you attend a church function as well; they're giving a great witness to their belief.

\* \* \*

*Characters:*
INTERVIEWER
JONAH PUSHER
MS. STURIL

*For list of props, see index, page 166.*

INT   I have news today that I know will excite many of you. Jonah Pusher, chairman of the state's board of education, has announced that school districts will now begin using—quote—modern Christian training methods—end quote—in the schools. This is great news for those of us who have feared educational institutions would indoctrinate our children with humanist values. Mr. Pusher has agreed to come today to talk about this dramatic development in secular education. . . .

*Enter Pusher, carrying several reports under his arm, followed by Ms. Sturil. Neither seems particu-*

*larly odd or outlandish—they should play their parts seriously, and not as if they hope to get laughs.*

INT   Welcome, Mr. Pusher, we appreciate your joining us.

PUSH   No problem! After all, it's thanks to Christians like many of the folks here that we've found the answer to our educational needs. And this is Janet Sturil, one of this state's finest teachers. She's been working in a pilot program to eliminate the bugs in this new system.

INT   What made you turn to Christian values in education?

PUSH   Well, we saw that the "modern methods" of many educators just weren't working. Now, don't get us wrong. We have many fine students who are learning well, but we can't deny we're also seeing problems.

INT   Such as?

STUR   Well, there's the violence that goes on, especially in the bigger districts.

PUSH   But in the smaller ones, as well.

STUR   True. And problems of student apathy, rebellion, hostility . . .

PUSH   . . . And, of course, with dropouts, that sort of thing. A special committee was formed to discuss ways of overcoming them.

STUR   That's when we began to take a hard look at how churches work.

PUSH   *[With a laugh]* After all, you never read about Sunday school teachers or youth leaders being knifed.

INT   That's true. But what made you turn to teaching Christian ethics, when the schools as a whole have been so careful to avoid even the mention of anything Christian?

STUR   That isn't exactly true. I've heard Jesus Christ mentioned every day where I teach. In the halls, the cafeteria, during games, and especially during tests.

INT   You hear students praying that often? Out loud?

STUR   Who said anything about praying?

PUSH   *[To Interviewer]* I think you're getting the wrong idea here. We aren't teaching the students Christian *ethics* . . . our curriculum remains the same. It's just our discipline methods that will follow the course of the modern Christians.

INT   Oh. How do you mean?

PUSH   It's very simple! Why do some students get rebellious? Why do some students fail classes, and others drop out? Obviously, they're rebelling against education because we've stuffed it down their throats.

STUR   We've forced it on them! No wonder some of them have turned against it.

INT   I don't understand. How does this fit in with Christian training?

PUSH   Well, we've seen that Christian families are very careful to avoid forcing religion on their children.

INT   But we try to teach our children Christian principles. We take them to church . . .

PUSH   . . . But you don't force them to take part in church activities or in youth ministries. And why?

INT   Because we're afraid it will make them rebel against religion.

PUSH   Exactly! The idea is wonderful. We call it Volunteer Basis Education. Now, we're not closing the schools, and we're not encouraging students to stay away. In fact, we'll encourage them to come. We're just not going to require it.

STUR   Yes. The teachers will come to work, the buses will go out, so if the students want to come, they can.

INT   And if they don't want to come?

PUSH   They don't have to!

INT   I can't imagine many students would come of their own will.

PUSH   Not at first, but why push them? They'd just grow up hating to learn! They'll resent people in authority, they'll resent reading books!

INT   At least they'll be *able* to read books.

PUSH   Look, when they're ready to learn, they'll show up. And when they do, they'll be ready to get serious. But first, some have got to sow their wild oats.

STUR   And another wonderful thing! Students who come will be given homework, but they'll only have to do it if they're in the mood. After all, we don't want them to grow up resenting homework.

INT   All this sounds like it would be disastrous.

PUSH   Oh, I don't know about that!

STUR   Our school district serves 1,500 students. I've been teaching the pilot program for a year now, and I'll have you know I have as many as 45 students!

INT   45 students attend your classes?

STUR   Yes! In . . . a manner . . . of speaking.

INT   What do you mean, in a manner of speaking?

STUR   (*Hesitating*) I had 45 students in *one* class.

INT   Which class?

STUR   The . . . uh . . . all-school assembly.

INT   You mean you only had 45 students attend school out of 1,500?

PUSH   I'm sure the others will come around.

INT   Don't you see what you're doing? Students are too young to be allowed to do only what *they* want to do! If you don't make them come and learn to read, they never will! They'll be too busy with their "fun" time activities!

PUSH   But eventually they'll be ready!

INT   It'll be too late! They'll be too set in their ways! You've got to start now! They won't know how to learn! You'll end up with adults who have no discipline, and who don't know anything that their parents did, or anything they need for life, because you never made them sit down long enough to really let it sink in!

PUSH   I never thought of that. *[To Sturil:]* I think we'd better go form a committee.

107

*He starts to leave, then stops and turns to the interviewer.*

PUSH   Can I ask you a question?

INT   Sure. Go ahead.

PUSH   Why do *you* use this method to teach Christianity?

*END*

# 19

# MANNA HELPER

"We remember the fish we ate in Egypt at no cost—also the cucumbers, melons, leeks, onions and garlic. But now we have lost our appetite; we never see anything but this manna!" (Num. 11:5–6).

In the musical play "Fiddler on the Roof," the beggar steps up to a wealthy butcher and asks for alms. The butcher proudly hands him a kopek, the Russian coin. "What!" the beggar moans. "One kopek? Last week you gave me two kopeks!"

"Well, I've had a bad week," the butcher patiently explains.

Dumbfounded, the beggar demands, "And for your misfortune, *I* should suffer?"

When God gives us a blessing or a gift, we're fond of prying open its mouth to count its teeth, or to bite down to see if it is real. The Israelites were like that when Moses led them out of Egypt and God provided them manna to eat. The disciples were the same when they got into scraps over who would be the greatest in the kingdom. We do it today, griping about our place in life when we should be whistling that old hymn, "Count your blessings, name them one by one/ Count your blessings, see what God has done."

This quick little skit is the very voice of God's selfish children.

\* \* \*

Characters:
MOTHER
FATHER
CHILDREN

ANNOUNCER (should be able to sing and play guitar)

*For list of props, see index, page 166.*

ANNOUNCER   Hey, man, are you gettin' tired of this scene?

MOTHER   Etam! Jezreel! Ishma! Idbash! Hazzelelponi! Time for dinner!

CHILDREN   What're we havin', Mommee?

MOTHER   [*Trying to sound impressive*] It's . . . *manna!*

OTHERS   Again! Yuck!

FATHER   Manna! Manna! Manna! Always manna! When are we going to have something that doesn't taste like school paste!

CHILDREN   What's school paste?

ANNOUNCER   Be cool, man! Don't get lost in the wilderness. We've got just the thing with Manna Helper! It's filled with all those things you miss so much and talk so much about since you went the somber way of the Lord—leeks and onions from the fertile Nile! Just mix it with that manna when no one's looking and your godly friends will never know! Manna Helper turns that yucky school paste into something... *WOW!*

FATHER   [*Hugging Mother*] Now that's what I call a meal!

MOTHER   Oh, Etam, you're such a tease!

ANNOUNCER   [*Singing and strumming guitar*]

Manna in the mornin',
Manna in the evenin',
Manna at-a suppah time!
Manna's so divine
When Manna Helper's on the
    line!

*END*

# 20

# THE QUICKER MORAL-UPPER

"Suppose a brother or sister is without clothes and daily food. If one of you says to him, 'Go, I wish you well; keep warm and well fed,' but does nothing about his physical needs, what good is it?" (James 2:15–16).

Everyone loves to supply a spiffy answer, a quick fix, a fast and clean involvement in another's suffering that leaves the helper feeling warm and gushy about himself, just like oatmeal.

But when your friends or family are really in need, they don't need your helpful imagery. They need your love and concern, they need your *time*.

We have so many help books today! Books to deal with every possible problem—failed love, loneliness, physical pain, financial disaster, grief—and it's so easy to run to the bookstore, snatch one up, and slap it in the sufferer's hands. "Here," we say, smiling, "this will really help you. I wish you well. Keep warm and fed. Hey, catch you later!"

Printed words are printed words. They can be helpful, but they'll never fill the void caused when people refuse to involve themselves. If you're suffering and a friend hands you a glitzy book, then disappears, it's a lot like getting a love letter addressed to "Occupant."

Yes, God sent us a book—the Bible. It helps us in every situation. But he knew we needed more. So he sent his Son to die for us. He in turn sent the Holy Spirit to teach us and guide us. And he left a twenty-four-hour prayer line open so that we can talk to him anytime.

Can we do the same for those *we* love?

\* \* \*

*Characters:*
    ROSIE
    ALICE
    MUFFIE

*For list of props, see index page 167.*

*A restaurant. A table down center and, on it, a cup of "coffee" (in reality it can be empty). Rosie is on stage, holding a cup of coffee (actually water). Alice enters, carrying a vase with goldenrod.*

ALICE    Rosie! I brought these flowers to celebrate the opening of your coffeehouse! What a wonderful ministry, and you look so busy!

ROSIE    How nice, Alice . . . ragweed.

ALICE    Oh, no . . . they're goldenrod! Do you like them?

ROSIE    They're nothing to sneeze about. Uh-oh, here comes Muffie from the church office, and she looks upset.

ALICE    Hi, Muffie! How are things going with that cute youth director you're dating?

MUFFIE    *[Crying hysterically]* Awwwooooo! I just found out he's . . . *gay!!*

*She begins to bawl all the harder.*

ROSIE    Muffie, watch out for that cup of . . . !

*Muffie knocks over a coffee cup and, mindless of her action, buries her head to wail.*

ALICE    Uh-oh, it'll take some hard counseling to clean up this spiritual mess.

ROSIE    Nonsense. It'll just take this.

*She takes a Daily Devotional from her apron.*

ALICE    A Daily Devotional?

ROSIE    No . . . !

*She rips it in half.*

ROSIE    Half a Daily Devotional! It's the Quicker Moral-Upper! The Daily Devotional is so strong, you can hand it to any spiritual mess and forget it. Even after I dip half of a Daily Devotional in this coffee, just watch how it handles Muffie.

MUFFIE    *[Disgusted by the soggy Daily Devotional]* Ooohhhh! *[Then, delighted by what she reads]* Oooohhhh!

ALICE    *[Raising her cup in a toast]* I've got to hand it to you, Rosie! You really handled that spiritual mess! *[Merrily, she sips from the Daily-Devotional-dunked cup.]*

ROSIE    *[Pulling another Daily Devotional from her apron and holding it before the audience]* Not me! The credit all goes to this. The Daily Devotional: It's the Quicker Moral-Upper!

*END*

# 21

# SPIRITUALLY FED

"These people come near to me with their mouth and honor me with their lips, but their hearts are far from me. Their worship of me is made up only of rules taught by men" (Isa. 29:13).

For some people, church is the ultimate pajama party. They come there to play, to feel popular, and maybe to catch a little sleep.

That's the attitude of the pastoral relations committee of the Coffin Corners Church. It's a problem many churches have. People get themselves appointed to committees where they can throw their weight around and gossip. They strut around looking important and holy. But when you scratch beneath the surface, you see they don't really care about working in the body of Christ or growing the least bit in their faith. When their baby-like faith is challenged too frequently by the pastor or a teacher, they want to toss him or her out.

Jesus had this trouble. Every time he turned around a crowd was wanting to throw him over a hill or stone him. His hometown folk saw his acts of power and they belittled him. The heads of the temple got so miffed with his challenging teaching that they plotted to have him crucified.

It's all too rare that a sleeping Christian, whose faith is challenged, says to himself, "Hey! I'd better wake up!"

There were a few men and women who woke up. They were called disciples and apostles. These guys were a tiny minority, but they heard the challenge, took it on, and turned the world upside down.

And those spiritual sleepers? They were still spiritually snoozing in Jerusalem when the Romans arrived to tear the city down.

* * *

*Characters:*
THE PASTORAL RELATIONS
  COMMITTEE:
    MRS. WILSON
    MR. SLOAN
    MRS. ROBERTS
    HARVEY
THE SUPERINTENDENT:
    REV. OTTERBEIN

*For list of props, see index, page 167.*

*Welcome to Rev. Otterbein's office. He is the superintendent of a conference—synod—whatever name is appropriate. A man of God, concerned with getting out the gospel, he has long ago learned the importance of holding his temper and getting along with his people. Patiently, he hears out every complaint. And today he is scheduled to hear the charges of the pastoral relations committee of the little church at Coffin Corners. The committee wants its pastor removed because, it says, it is not being spiritually fed.*

*Set: Rev. Otterbein's office. His desk, and enough chairs for each member of the committee to sit in conference with him—one chair sets beside the desk and one behind it. There are a few books on the desk, perhaps; a family portrait and a tasteful statuette suggest a mild-mannered, warmhearted man. Throughout the play, we watch this pleasant person collapse into a shivering, nervous wreck as he deals with this committee of psychos.*

*Enter Rev. Otterbein. He roots through the mess on his desk until he finds his calendar.*

REV    Calendar, calendar, calendar . . . ah! Calendar! *[He leafs through it, muttering the day's date over and over until he finds it.]* Ah! Here we are. Today I meet with the pastoral relations committee of the Coffin Corners Church regarding their request that I remove their pastor. Why do they want me to do that? Oh yes . . . they say they're not being spiritually fed. Hmm. That's odd. Rev. Waters always struck me as a dedicated and godly man.

*Enter the committee. Well . . . three of them. Harvey will be late. These are the folk who have held their church as a mighty fortress against the neighborhood for years. They have walked right in, without knocking, and up to Otterbein's desk. He looks up to discover them standing there.*

WILSON    Reverend Otterbein!

REV    *[Ironically]* Please, no need to knock, just come right in. *[He offers his hand to her]* How do you do . . . ! *[She ignores it, and the committee members help themselves to the chairs. After they have done so, he asks:]* Why don't you all have a seat?

*Sloan—gruff and angry—sits like a bad imitation of Churchill. Wilson, a self-appointed aristocrat, keeps her fingers clasped over her purse. Roberts is just a trifle daft and armed with an endearing smile. She whips her knitting out of a bag and goes to town:*

it is a sock that is six feet long and growing. We hear the endless clicking of her needles throughout the skit, and she only occasionally looks up from her work. They are strange characters, but they are nothing compared to Harvey—who has yet to enter.*

REV    *[Standing up and moving among them]* I welcome you to my humble office . . .

WILSON    It *is* a rather small office for a superintendent.

REV    *[Laughing]* At least you can see I'm not wasting conference funds on opulence!

SLOAN    Running for bishop, are you?

ROBERTS    *[To Mrs. Wilson]* Shouldn't you introduce us to the Reverend?

WILSON    Of course, dear. This is Mr. Sloan, a fine upstanding man in our little church, and this is Mrs. Roberts.

ROBERTS    That's a very nice statue on your desk.

REV    Why, thank you . . .

SLOAN    *[The eternal grouch]* I suppose our apportionments paid for it.

REV    *[Smiling in spite of it all]* Let's get to the matter at hand—namely, your problem with Rev. Waters.

ROBERTS    *[Sweetly, with just a touch of snideness]* Oh. Excuse *us* for being friendly.

WILSON    Now, now, Agnes. I'm sure the superintendent means nothing. He's under a good deal of stress, having to face us after he sent us that man. We must show mercy and charity.

SLOAN    *[Scoffing]* Charity! Pshaw!

ROBERTS  She meant charity in the "King James" sense, George.

SLOAN  I knew that.

REV  You state in your letter that Rev. Waters is not speaking the Word of God, and quite frankly I'm surprised, because . . .

WILSON  Are you calling us liars?

SLOAN  Anything to get himself off the hook!

REV  Of course I'm not! I'm just suggesting that perhaps you've not given him enough of a chance. Or perhaps you've misread him . . .

WILSON  We do *not* misread.

REV  [Aside] I'm surprised you read at all.

WILSON  What?

REV  Nothing.

SLOAN  [Taking out a cigarette] Do you mind if I smoke?

REV  I'd . . . prefer you didn't. I'm asthmatic.

SLOAN  Oh! Lovely! Ladies, our superintendent is one of those tongues speakers!

ROBERTS  [Mortified, to Wilson:] He's not going to start all that babbling now, is he?

REV  [An answer to her question, but also a prayerful plea against this ignorance, as he buries his face in his hands] No! [He notices for the first time the huge, woolly growth Roberts is creating.] What *is* that you're knitting?

ROBERTS  [Proudly] A sock.

REV  [As kindly as he can] It's at least six feet long.

ROBERTS  It's so hard to stop, once you've started. Sugar! I've lost count. [She begins to tear out a row.]

REV  Could one of you explain to me more fully what you mean by not being spiritually fed?

SLOAN  Rev. Waters is spiritually immature. He plays basketball with our youth.

ROBERTS  He's driving us to financial ruin! He closed down our Daughters of Oliver Cromwell Raffle!

REV  What has this got to do with spiritual food?

WILSON  How about this? We leave the church feeling *guilty*.

REV  Guilty!

SLOAN  Finally! He agrees with something!

ROBERTS  [Shaking her head] And you said he'd never listen!

SLOAN  Of course he listens now. He's running for bishop!

WILSON  I've always felt it's important for a sermon to make you feel good about yourself. Rev. Waters' hardly ever do that.

REV  Perhaps he's trying to challenge you to a stronger commitment in your Christian life. To, as Paul says, make "living sacrifices" of yourselves.

SLOAN  Living sacrifice! We've *given* God a church! It wasn't cheap!

115

WILSON   And we've remodeled. What more does God want!

ROBERTS   [*Meaningfully*] We *used* to give him hymnbooks and furniture with memorial plaques. But that was in the days when the Daughters of Oliver Cromwell were allowed to hold a raffle.

REV   [*Trying a different tack*] Does Rev. Waters preach the Word? Does he use Scripture to back up his Sunday morning sermons?

WILSON   Probably not.

REV   [*After a doubletake*] *Probably* not?

WILSON   Well, I've . . . never heard him myself, actually. I spend Sunday mornings in the nursery. If I'm not going to be fed, I might as well feed the babies.

ROBERTS   [*Laughing*] Cookie! Your jokes are darling. [*To Rev*] You should hear how she talks about the songleader.

WILSON   Agnes!

REV   [*To Sloan*] Have *you* heard his Sunday sermons?

SLOAN   [*Blustering*] How can I! I run the sound system!

REV   Then you should hear them best of all!

SLOAN   It's hot up there! I usually fall asleep. Besides, it's the only chance I have to catch up on my Louis Lamour novels.

ROBERTS   Well, don't look at me. I use the sermon time to work on my sock. Sugar! [*And she begins ripping out a row.*]

REV   [*Not believing he's hearing this*] What about Sunday evening? His Wednesday Bible studies? Have you listened to him *then*?

*All three look at him as if he's asked a supremely stupid question.*

WILSON   Rev. Otterbein! We're *busy* people!

REV   [*Growing angry*] How can a pastoral relations committee sit here and tell me they're not being spiritually fed when none of them have even heard the pastor speak?

SLOAN   What do you take us for! Of course one of us has heard him speak!

REV   WHO?

WILSON   [*As if explaining to a child*] The chairman.

ROBERTS   You know! Harvey!

WILSON   He's attended every sermon and study Rev. Waters has given, and *he* says we aren't being spiritually fed.

SLOAN   He should know. He practically lives in that church.

WILSON   Such a godly man! You have to drag him away at the end of a service!

ROBERTS   Literally.

REV   Why isn't he here?

SLOAN   He IS here!

WILSON   He's a little shy. So he's waiting in the car.

ROBERTS    We'd have to drag him in to see you. Literally.

REV    *[Not liking the sound of this, but being brave]* Do that.

*Wilson and Sloan glance at one another, then rise and exit.*

ROBERTS    Sugar! *[She begins tearing out a row, and starts in again.]*

*For a moment, Rev. Otterbein and Mrs. Roberts share the stage. We can tell by Rev. Otterbein's look that he is wondering if things can get any crazier.*

*They do. For Mrs. Wilson and Mr. Sloan return, dragging Harvey between them. Harvey is indeed quite shy. For, you see, Harvey is dead. You'll never hear this committee admit that. Indeed, it is very defensive of its chairman. One suspects, however, that, deep down, they know his condition. They dump Harvey in the chair closest to the superintendent's desk, and his head thumps down onto the desktop. For a moment, Rev. Otterbein just stares.*

REV    Is he . . . asleep?

SLOAN    Of course not! He's just shy.

WILSON    Harvey? This is Rev. Otterbein. He has some questions for you.

*Sloan raises Harvey's right hand toward Rev. Otterbein.*

ROBERTS    *[Not looking up]* He says it's awfully nice to meet you.

*A little stunned, Rev shakes the limp hand.*

REV    It's ice-cold!

WILSON    He's usually much warmer, but the heater in the car broke.

ROBERTS    He'll warm up to you. Just keep hanging on.

*Rev lets go. The hand falls to the desk.*

SLOAN    Well! Ask away!

*Rev is now convinced he is dealing with dangerous people.*

REV    Harvey . . . ? Have you heard Rev. Waters' sermons?

WILSON    He says yes.

REV    I . . . didn't hear him respond.

SLOAN    Of course not. He doesn't speak. He just shakes his head. Harvey! Rev. Otterbein wants to know if you've heard Rev. Waters' sermons!

*Wilson takes Harvey by the hair, shakes his head yes, then releases it. With a thump, it clunks back onto the table.*

SLOAN    See? He said yes.

ROBERTS    Harvey is a very decisive man. Sugar. *[She begins to rip out a row.]*

REV    *[Feeling for a pulse]* This man is dead.

WILSON    Nonsense. He's just quiet.

SLOAN    Don't you have another question?

REV    Uh . . . Harvey . . . are you being spiritually fed?

*Wilson shakes Harvey's head no. Rev stares.*

117

WILSON   He says no.

REV   This is ridiculous. Mrs. Wilson! Mr. Sloan! Mrs. Roberts! Harvey is dead!

WILSON   [Looking closely at the head she holds between her hands] Harvey! Did you hear that?

SLOAN   He's as alive as anyone on our committee!

REV   [Holding a metal letter opener under Harvey's nose] Look at this! No mist!

WILSON   He's holding his breath. That's all.

ROBERTS   [Sweetly] He does it remarkably well.

SLOAN   Harvey! Tell Rev. Otterbein! You're alive, aren't you! [Wilson takes Harvey by the hair again and shakes his head yes.]

REV   [Shouting] Let him go and see if he answers!

WILSON   Fine! I will!

She does. Harvey's reaction is predictable: he collapses with a thump onto the desk, staring sightlessly at the audience. Strangely, Harvey doesn't say a word. Mrs. Wilson lifts one of his arms and lets it go. It flaps lifelessly to his side.

WILSON   [To Sloan] He does seem a trifle . . . loose, doesn't he?

ROBERTS   [Concentrating on her knitting] He used to be a little stiff about the joints. But then we enrolled him in aerobics!

REV   [A little maniacally] A-ha-ha-ha-ha-ha!

WILSON   I'll admit he's been a little . . . unresponsive during the readings. And I suppose it

might explain why he abstains so often on the board.

SLOAN   Not to mention that funny smell during the heat wave last August.

WILSON   And all those big, hunchbacked birds that we had to keep driving away at the church picnic.

SLOAN   [Sniffling a little] Poor Harvey. Now I'm sorry I yelled at him for missing that last pop-up at the softball game.

WILSON   Still, this doesn't change the fact we're spiritually unfed!

REV   [Completely freaking out] What! Are you crazy! Of course you're not spiritually fed! You never listen to a word the pastor says! [To Wilson] You're off feeding babies the same milk you've been drinking for years! [To Sloan] You're up in some booth reading Duke Wayne novels! [To Roberts] And you've spent the last thirty years knitting a sock for a snake! Meanwhile Harvey is dead! You cannot "feed" a corpse! A corpse does not eat! You could stuff STEAK down his throat and it would just pop back out of his mouth!!

ROBERTS   [Thoughtfully] That would explain the awful mess at the chili dinner.

REV   [Shrieking] GET OUT OF HERE! AND TAKE HARVEY WITH YOU!!

SLOAN   See if you get my vote at conference this year!

WILSON   I suspect this meeting has reached an impasse.

They take Harvey by the ankles and leave. Roberts sits, continuing to knit, until she miscounts again.

ROBERTS    Sugar.

*And with that she takes up her knitting and exits. Rev sits, gathering the shreds of his sanity. He chances a look heavenward.*

REV    Lord, with this kind of sheep in the flock, why does the devil bother with wolves?

### END

*Director's Note: This skit involves "stage violence"—that is, poor Harvey is dragged across stage, and his head is thumped around like a basketball on a stick. There's a trick to this: first, make sure he's wearing such clothes as will protect him from rug burn—suspenders will help keep his shirt tucked in and his pants from slipping off! Most importantly, when Harvey's head is being manipulated by Mrs. Wilson, just have the actress playing Wilson take a loose hold of his hair and leave her arm limp—and the actor playing Harvey will control all these movements himself. In this manner, it will still look as if she is controlling the action, but will eliminate the likelihood of injury to Harvey's innocent hair follicles.*

# 22

# WHAT'S THE ANSWER?

"Dear friends, let us love one another, for love comes from God. Everyone who loves has been born of God and knows God" (1 John 4:7).

What's the biggest single point of Christianity? "God is love." We are not to confuse that with "love is God," as some people do. But God's greatest emotion is love. His greatest acts are the result of his love. And so we are expected to copy that same virtue: love one another. If we do, we show Christ.

The world has always recognized the need for love. Coca-Cola® did a big commercial about it some years back. The Beatles made a fortune singing, "All you need is love." So why do we keep ending up with hate and war?

It's because the world doesn't know the *kind* of love it needs—the love that Jesus brings us. Here is a skit about some youth discussing the question, "What's the answer to all the hate and war?" They come upon the perfect formula: God's love equals peace on earth, and peace in our souls.

*An informal interview format—the youth leader (YL) talks with three youths—all four sit in comfortable looking chairs, sipping pop. Downstage or to one side, however, there are two or four actors acting out a minor scene or two.*

*As a suggestion, you might find this a good piece to use as a video project, either videotaping the entire play, or simply videotaping the Crusader-Moslem fight and the parables, then playing them on a big-screen TV at the appropriate times.*

* * *

**Characters:**
  YOUTH LEADER (YL)
  YOUTH 1
  YOUTH 2
  YOUTH 3
2–8 Actors, playing:
  CRUSADER
  MOSLEM/INFIDEL
  VICTIM
  HOOD(S)
  EVANGELIST
  DEACON
  ARAB

*For list of props, see index, page 167.*

YL  Man has always had neighbors, but has he ever known how to deal with them? Whether they're the folks next door or the guys across the border, or even that guy in the horn-rimmed glasses across from you in the living room, people just don't seem to get along. Oh, we do on the surface—we talk and trade and play together. But the minute a disagreement comes up . . .

CRUSADER  We must show these infidels the power of a loving God!

MOSLEM  We will teach them to invade the Holy Land!

*Like two comical tanks, and to the tune of the "Chinese Dance" segment of* Nutcracker Suite, *they charge one another and fight—finally killing each other off.*

YOUTH 1    There must be a better way!

YL    So what's the answer?

YOUTH 1    Got me. The whole world's gone crazy.

YOUTH 2    Tell me about it!

YOUTH 3    Every New Year's Eve when that Times Square ball hits the ground, I just say, "Thank God, I've survived another 365."

YOUTH 2    We're on borrowed time.

YOUTH 3    It isn't like we're any crazier than we were a thousand years ago. I mean, look at Nero. And Herod—he was mad as the Hatter! Look at Genghis Khan!

YOUTH 1    The difference now is, all those crazies can put the whole world in a war.

YOUTH 2    And some of them have nuclear bombs.

YL    Can America keep world peace?

YOUTH 2    We can't even keep American peace! Our cities are killing fields!

YOUTH 1    Every time you stick your head out the door you risk becoming tomorrow's headline.

YOUTH 2    *[Showing newspaper]* Yeah. Get this: "Woman stabbed 28 times."

YOUTH 3    *[Pointing out another headline]* Or this one: "Woman Shoots Husband in Domestic Struggle."

YOUTH 2    See? You don't even have to stick your head out the door. Just stick it in the kitchen and say, "Honey, you burned the roast!"

YOUTH 1    Between countries, in the streets, at home—people just don't get along. Things are so intense no one can cope, and everybody's stressed out.

YL    So you're saying we'll never get along?

YOUTH 1    Countries won't get along with each other until they can get along with themselves.

YOUTH 3    And how can you get along with the stranger next door when you can't get along with your own family?

YOUTH 2    Hey, forget the family. Most people can't even get along with themselves.

YL    So what do you do?

YOUTH 2    Yeah, what *do* you do?

YL    Try this on: Two thousand years ago God came to earth in the form of a man. He told his followers that if there was ever going to be peace among men, it would have to start with perfect love.

YOUTH 2    And perfect love begins with Christ. Right?

YOUTHS 1 & 3    *[Applauding, just a bit snide]* Hey! Right on! Smart dude, man! *[Etc.]*

YOUTH 1    And now, the million dollar question: where did Jesus talk about the perfect relationship?

YOUTH 3   Easy! The Good Samaritan. It's in Luke. This lawyer guy says to Jesus, "Teacher, what must I do to inherit eternal life?"

YOUTH 2   And Jesus answers the guy with another question.

YOUTH 3   He did that a lot.

YOUTH 2   "What is written in the law?"

YOUTH 1   "That you shall love the Lord your God with all your heart, with all your soul, with all your strength, and with all your mind; and that you shall love your neighbor as yourself."

YOUTH 2   "You have answered right. Do this and you will live forever."

YOUTH 3   "But who is my neighbor?"

YOUTH 1   I can take it from here!

YL   Go for it!

YOUTH 2   *[With a groan]* I can hardly wait!

*As the story unwinds, the downstage actors act it out.*

YOUTH 1   *[A Rod Serling imitation]* Imagine that you've worked hard all week, saving every penny so you can spend tonight cruising for the babes. You've waxed your Trans Am till it glows, and you're dressed to a T. Off you drive, the wind whipping through your open windows. Then you draw to a stop at a traffic light in the outskirts of Skuztown. Suddenly hoods armed with crowbars and penny-filled socks surround your car. You have entered . . . *The Good Samaritan Zone!*

YOUTHS 2 & 3   *[They sing the Twilight Zone theme.]*

YOUTH 1   You're dragged bodily from your car. Fists fly in the dark, landing in the soft pit of your stomach. You feel the crack of a crowbar across your back. Finally they dump you in the alley. Having taken your money and your clothes . . .

YOUTH 2   Oooh! NC-17!

YOUTH 1    . . . They speed away in your car.

YOUTH 2   My turn! *[Suddenly, he is a Bible-thumper.]* Now by chance, my brethren, an evangelist was going down the road; and he heareth a voice; and that voice, it calleth him from the dark alley, crying, "Help-a! Help-a!" The evangelist, being filled with the Spirit of love, stopped in his tracks and cocketh his head in thus manner saying, "Hark! A voice calleth me from the dark! Indeed, it is a poor, lost sheep in need of physical aid!" But the evangelist, he looketh around and, seeing there were many shadows possibly hideth-ing many hoods, he said, "What knoweth I of first aid? I shall remember to pray for him!" And, crossing the street, he wenteth his way.

YOUTH 3   So likewise a church deacon saw him lying naked and he said, "Can a man who dresses like that give a decent offering? For, if he can't afford clothes, certainly he can't afford the collection plate. Why, I doubt he even attends my church." And so saying, the deacon also crossed the road and went his way.

YOUTH 1   But then a . . . uhm . . . *[Aside, to the others]* Quick! What's a good modern-day equivalent to a Samaritan?

YL   It would have to be someone traditionally looked down upon. . . .

YOUTH 3   An ethnic minority!

123

YOUTH 1   Too broad.

YOUTH 2   A terrorist!

YOUTH 3   Saddam Hussein!

YOUTH 1   Too extreme.

VICTIM   Somebody help me!

YOUTH 3   Say *some*one!

YOUTH 1   But a, uh . . . Libyan-Iraqi foreign exchange student who ate tuna that cost the lives of dolphins and who favored killing whales came to where the victim was. And when he saw him, he had compassion. He gave him some drink.

ARAB   Salaam, my friend.

VICTIM   Espresso?

YOUTH 1   . . . And bound his wounds with 547 Band-Aids. He even took him to the emergency room, where he slipped the doctor enough money to pay for his entire hospitalization.

YOUTH 2   You've got to be kidding.

YOUTH 1   He owns an oil field.

YOUTH 2   Oh.

YL   So which was the man's neighbor?

YOUTHS 1, 2 & 3   [*Dutifully*] The one who showed mercy on him.

YL   So if we show mercy, we'll all get along?

YOUTH 3   Well . . . there's a little more than that. For instance, the Golden Rule.

YOUTH 1   "Do unto others as you would have them do unto you."

YOUTH 2   It takes understanding.

YOUTH 1   Most of all, it takes time.

YOUTH 3   No, most of all it takes love.

YL   Ah! "Love your neighbors as you love yourself."

YOUTH 2   And if you don't love yourself?

YOUTH 1   Then your neighbor's got troubles.

YOUTH 3   How can you love anyone else if you can't love or respect yourself?

YL   So if you don't love yourself right now, how do you come to do it?

YOUTH 1   It takes time. You recognize your good points, your talents. You remember there's a definite place for you in the universe.

YOUTH 3   In God's plans, as it were. And having Christ in your life can make all the difference in the world.

YOUTH 2   Come on! I know a lot of people who aren't Christians and they're happy. They love themselves, and they have lots of love for others.

YOUTH 1   And I know even more nonChristians who are completely miserable. Look, I was happy before I became a Christian. But I'm even happier now. I've got something extra.

YOUTH 2   [*Singing*] Hallelujah! Hallelujah!

YOUTH 1   Anyway, first you accept yourself. Then you can start getting along with your friends and your family. And *then* you can start caring for all those people you don't personally know.

YOUTH 2    I'm not sure I follow.

YOUTH 3    That's where Jesus comes in.

YL    Right. You begin to feel his perfect love, and it grows until you can love beyond yourself, even beyond the people you know, until you can love the whole world.

YOUTH 2    Seems kind of unlikely to me.

YOUTH 3    I think it's a good goal to have. The world can't clean up its act unless each of its members do, one at a time.

YOUTH 1    So the real question is, how do you clean up your own act? How do you find peace in yourself?

YL    So how do you? What's the answer?

YOUTH 1    Love.

YOUTH 3    Love and Jesus.

YOUTH 2    Perfect love.

YOUTH 1    So, hey, we've just solved the world's problems! What do we do for an encore?

ALL    PIZZA!

YL    Sounds good to me.

*All exit.*

*END*

# 23

# THE REUNION

"The prayer of a righteous man is powerful and effective" (James 5:16b).

There are three important steps toward bringing your friends to Jesus:

1. *Tell them about Jesus.* That doesn't mean you should slap a Bible on their desk, open it to John 3:16, and push their noses into the binding until the truth and the ink sink in. It means you tell them—at the right time—that Jesus loves them, cares for them, and died for them. It means you invite them to youth group, hear them out, and be ready to tell them about sin and Jesus' forgiveness and lead them to him when you know they're ready to hear it, or when they ask.

2. *Show them about Jesus.* It doesn't do to tell them what Jesus has done for you, then sneak out of your house late at night to attend an off-limits party. Live a Christian life, refusing to take part in things you know compromise your faith. Be consistent. Don't be fatalistic, don't be negative (but don't be so happy and cheery that it becomes an act). Be their trustworthy confidant and shoulder to cry on.

3. *Tell Jesus about them.* He knows already, of course. But he wants to hear how much you care. Pray every day for their salvation. If they don't become Christians right away, or even for many years, don't give up. Keep praying. Jesus' brother, James, pointed out how powerful patient prayer can be. Many people will go to heaven not seeing their children or friends become Christians, but their prayer is still working, nudging those loved ones along. And there are some really surprising reunions going on between those who have prayed and those who have become answers to never-say-die prayer warriors. For example, witness the reunion of Sam and Kirk one heavenly day.

* * *

**Characters:**
SAM
KIRK

*A seemingly wonderful day . . . fact is, the day couldn't be better. On stage: a bench—the kind you might see in a park. Kirk enters, whistling "Just Another Day In Paradise." He carries a huge book. He sits on the bench and begins to browse over the book happily. He sees something in it that he likes.*

KIRK   Hey, hey, Frank! Way to go!

*Again, he reads a few moments. Again, his eyes light up.*

KIRK   Arlene, you old bat! I knew you could do it!

*He starts to cry a little, because Kirk is a real emotional type.*

KIRK    [Sniffs] This is great. Just great!

*He immerses himself in the book completely. Along comes Sam, grinning, apparently looking for someone. He finds Kirk and sneaks up behind, then claps his hands over Kirk's eyes.*

SAM    Kirk Masters, this is your life! Do you recognize the following voice from your past? [He now speaks in the voice of a child.] "Mr. Masters, you'll never ketch me lettin' air outta your tires agin!"

KIRK    [Amazed] Wait! I know that voice . . . I know . . . Sammy! Little Sammy Jessup!

SAM    [Shouting excitedly] Yes!

*Kirk jumps up and bounces back and forth for joy. Sam does the same.*

KIRK    Little Sammy! I never thought I'd see you here!

SAM    I'm surprising a *lot* of people!

KIRK    I just can't believe it!

SAM    Hey! You really remember me? After all these years?

KIRK    Come on, who could forget little Sammy the Freak? You were a nightmare. [Sniffs]

SAM    [Patting his shoulder as they sit] Aw, Kirk, don't go cryin' now!

KIRK    Man! It's been so long since I've seen you, kid! Last time I saw you, you were what? Sixteen?

SAM    Yeah, about there. And you were what, a hunnerd an' ten?

KIRK    [Laughs] Yeah, old as Moses' toes, you always said.

SAM    We said that, didn't we?

KIRK    "Old man Moses," you always said when I passed the offering plate. "Hey, old man Moses! Fall on your face!"

SAM    Yeah, I remember that!

KIRK    Then you'd stick out your foot and trip me goin' down the aisle.

SAM    [Embarrassed] Yeah . . . I, uh, remember that.

KIRK    Yeah, you were a wild one. Kickin' and swearing a blue streak in Sunday school, as long as you went. You stole the stuffin's out of my store, bullied the little boys on the block. I remember that time you snuck into the Salvation Army Thanksgiving Day dinner. Restuffed the turkeys with worms, and plugged up the holes with the original stuffing. Old Mrs. Winkle was the one to discover it. She hauled a leg off a little too vigorous and those wigglers just tumbled out. Course, they weren't wiggly then, a little too fried.

SAM    I know! I was watchin' through the window! Half the people cleared out right there!

KIRK    Mrs. Winkle was so surprised she lost her uppers in the yams! That's when the other half left.

SAM    Yeah, I lived to regret it. Wait a minute! I thought I covered myself well on that one! You knew it was me?

KIRK    Not 'til now!

*They both laugh.*

SAM   Yeah. I did a lot of bad to you, too, Kirk.

KIRK   *[Waving him off]* Aaaah!

SAM   Really! I shot rocks through your windows, dumped fertilizer on your carpet, rebuilt your Studebaker on top of your garage. Hey! Stand up! I want a good look at you!

KIRK   You, too! You, too!

*They stand and look each other over.*

SAM   Kirk, this is great! That awful limp you had's gone!

KIRK   What do you expect in this place! You got so big!

SAM   You got so . . . young!

KIRK   It happens, Sam! It happens!

*They stand, unbelieving, each trying to say something, and neither able to do so. Finally:*

KIRK   Well, hey, welcome to heaven, Sam!

SAM   Glad to be here!

*They clasp again, hugging and laughing. Kirk begins to cry.*

KIRK   This is great! Just great!

SAM   Hey! Hey, hey, hey! None of that here! Say, what were you readin' there?

KIRK   *[Taking up the book]* It's the newest edition of "Additions to the Book of Life."

SAM   Oh yeah?

KIRK   Sure! They put out an edition every other week or so. Marty, down at the print shop . . .

SAM   Marty?

KIRK   Marty Luther. *Martin* Luther.

SAM   *The* Martin Luther?

KIRK   Oh, yeah. Great guy. He and Chuck Wesley mostly write songs there and turn 'em out, but he handles the Book of Life Additions, too. 'Course, with the revivals going on in Korea and Africa and those places, they can't turn out a real up-to-date one fast enough, so they just run the names of the folks that are on their way up.

SAM   Yeah? And you read it? The whole thing?

KIRK   Religiously. Hey, I read obituaries every day of my life. Why stop now? Besides, it's so nice to read someone's left that old world and is comin' home. And sometimes I get a nice surprise. I see someone I know. Hey! Why haven't I seen your name the past couple of days?

SAM   I've been here two years now.

KIRK   Two years! And I ain't seen you till now?

SAM   I'd've come by sooner, honest. But, Jesus came and met me, put his arms right around me and just held me close, man! I just sat in his presence, praisin' and grinnin' all that time! I'm figurin' to go back for another couple years after I visit you.

KIRK   Maybe I'll join you! Wait. I didn't read about you two years ago, either.

SAM   Sure you did. You just didn't know it. I . . . uh . . . changed my last name after I got out of prison.

KIRK  Prison. Always figured you'd wind up there.

SAM  Yeah. I needed money so I hit a grocery store and the robbery went bad. Press made a real case of it.

KIRK  [Happily again] Aw, forget it! You obviously repented, so it don't matter now! [He looks at Book] Look! Remember Annie Worth?

SAM  . . . Annie . . .

KIRK  Blonde hair. Nice personality. Prom Queen, '56.

SAM  The one with the great legs!

KIRK  Nice teeth, too.

There is a pause.

KIRK  I always was a teeth man.

SAM  Yeah! Sure, I remember her! We went together for a while. She went by her middle name, Rae, then. Yeah! She went to a revival at the church one day. She went down to the altar.

KIRK  [Proudly] I took her down myself. Right there she dropped everything bad in her life.

SAM  Including me.

KIRK  [Quickly] Course, it was the pastor who counseled her.

SAM  So Annie Rae is comin' here? What a surprise I'll be to her! She'll go through the roof!

KIRK  We can do that, now.

SAM  Yeah, we can!

KIRK  [Happily] Says here she was in an accident and died on the operating table.

SAM  Great!

KIRK  Fantastic!

They jump to their feet and dance in circles, singing childlike:

BOTH  Annie's died and gone to heaven! Annie's died and gone to heaven!

SAM  [Noticing something in the book, he picks it up.] Oh, hey, wait: look here. There's a correction.

KIRK  A correction?

SAM  Yeah . . . listen: "Near-death experience, but pulled back." [Sadly] They got her heart goin' again.

KIRK  [Sadly, tearing up] She's such a wonderful woman, and she's going to pull through! This is terrible!

SAM  [Patting him on the shoulder] Hey! Hey! Come on, no tears, remember? No tears up here!

KIRK  You're right. You're right. It's just that . . . death can be so unfair.

SAM  Cheer up! She'll die sooner or later! Nobody lives forever! [á la V-8:] What am I saying? Of course they do.

KIRK  So. How was your trip?

SAM  Easy. I went in my sleep.

KIRK  How'd it happen? I must have prayed for you every day, but man, when I died, you were on a hot road for hell.

SAM  I hated you when I was a kid.

KIRK  Yeah.

SAM  You were so nice! Never an angry word! I did everything I could to get you mad! But I couldn't do it! I couldn't get one four-letter word out of you!

KIRK  You sure wore a lot of knee holes into my britches, though.

SAM  I know. Drove me crazy! You always had a good word for me. It didn't make sense. I wanted so bad for you to hate me. Remember Furball? You'd always sit on the porch, her on your lap, scratchin' her ears.

KIRK  Crazy old cat. I even let her eat at the table. She was all I had after Ella died.

SAM  I was in my roadster one day and saw that fool animal down in the road, and you on the porch. All I could think of was the look you'd have on your face and the hate you'd have in your heart if I made that thing into a pancake. I never forgot that day.

KIRK  You must have thought I was a real fool, a grown man, kneelin' by a dead cat, an' cryin' like that.

SAM  I thought you were absolutely crazy. I was waitin' for you to look up at me. Waitin' to see that same hate in your eyes I had in mine. I was gonna laugh in your face, flip you the bird and fly. But when you looked up, you weren't cryin' for the cat. You were cryin' for me!

KIRK  [Quietly] I said, "God loves you, boy."

SAM  I won't repeat what I said to you. Then I hightailed it.

KIRK  A few nights later you busted up my store. They took you to reform school and I never saw you again. Read about you once in a while. None of it good. But I never let you go, boy. Night after night I prayed for you. Right to my dying day.

SAM  Yeah. Years later I found myself in the pen. I'd been in reform school, but this was hard time. With killers and rapists. I tried to be nice to everybody. This lifer, they called him Samson, he didn't like me anyway. I was scared to death of him. Did everything I could to make him like me, stayed out of his way, and he just hated me even more. Always grabbed me and beat me up. Then one day in the shop he busted my head with a pipe. I fell down, grabbed my head . . . I pulled my fingers away and they were red with blood. And blood was stinging my eyes. And then I saw his feet step in front of me, and I knew he was standing there, just waiting for me to look up at him, just waiting to see the fear in my eyes. And I looked up. And all I could think of was a crazy man with a pancake cat and I suddenly said, "God loves you, boy."

*There is a pause.*

SAM  Next time I woke up I was in the infirmary. I started cryin' like a baby. A week later these prison ministry guys led me to the Lord.

KIRK  That's great!

SAM  When I got out, I came back to town and asked where I could find you. They showed me the stone. "Gone Home," it said. I found me a good church, Kirk, and started a prison ministry. One day we were talkin' about what Bible heroes we most looked forward to meeting when we got to heaven, and why. One guy said David, another said Paul. Samson—I led him to the Lord—he said, "I want to see Samson . . . 'cause I got his name. And 'cause, even after he spent a life being stupid, God forgave him. Who do you want to see, Sam?" And I said, "Gotta be Moses. 'Cause he was on his face lovin' and prayin' for his people even when they squashed his cat."

*During a silent moment, he sits beside Kirk and smiles.*

SAM    [*To Kirk*] Thanks, Moses. I love ya.

*They embrace.*

*END*

# 24

# ICE MEN

"Blessed are you when people insult you, persecute you and falsely say all kinds of evil against you because of me. Rejoice and be glad, because great is your reward in heaven, for in the same way they persecuted the prophets who were before you" (Matt. 5:11–12).

The story is true: during the Roman persecutions the believers of a town were hauled out of their homes in the dead of winter and shoved onto the surface of a frozen lake. Soldiers surrounded them—if the victims tried to come in off the ice they would be killed. The Roman officer offered them their lives in return for what he considered to be an easy price. All they had to do was deny their faith in Jesus. Then they could come off the ice and go home, free men and women.

Instead, nearly every person remained on the ice, singing hymns until they literally froze to death. This moving and beautiful witness was so powerful that one Roman soldier took off his armor, went out on the ice, and sat with the people until he, too, died for his newfound faith.

Suffering is a terrible thing, and God doesn't wish it on us. But when it comes, he will often use it to strengthen our love for him, and as a way to lead others to him.

\* \* \*

*Characters:*
  TWO ROMAN SOLDIERS:
    LUCIUS
    VITO

*For list of props, see index, page 166.*

*It is apparently winter, for the soldiers are wrapped in blankets and sit before an imaginary fire. They are intently watching the subjects they are guarding—a group of Christians, standing on the ice in the middle of a small lake. These Christians are, in reality, the audience.*

LUCIUS    Idiots.

VITO    [*Puffing into the air*] You can see your breath.

LUCIUS    [*Astonished*] They sit and they stand out there, singing hymns through their chattering teeth.

VITO    Of course you can see your breath! It's the dead of winter.

LUCIUS    From the looks of it, I should guess a couple have died, Vito. That woman over there hasn't moved in an hour. And that old man. He's blue.

VITO    I suppose he is, Lucius. If they were more practical, these Christians, they'd take his clothes off him to help keep someone else warm.

LUCIUS    Idiots!

VITO    Of course, if they were *really* practical, they'd just march in here off that ice, deny their Jesus, and be free to go home.

LUCIUS    How long have they been there?

VITO    All day. Since before dawn and now the sun is setting. I'm cold myself. They must be freezing. I wouldn't sit out there and freeze my backside off for my gods. Let the gods freeze their own backsides, that's what I'd say.

LUCIUS    What kind of people are they? What kind of people do that?

VITO    You've been sitting there and answering that all day long.

LUCIUS    *[Nodding]* Idiots.

VITO    Idiots!

LUCIUS    In the middle of the night we roust them out of their village and kill their teachers. Still they cling to their god. Then we haul off their youngest children for slaves. They begin to pray. General Janus takes the lot of them and hauls them out into the middle of this frozen lake.

VITO    General Janus surrounds the lake with soldiers and tells the Christians all they have to do to come off the lake is denounce their Christ. "Think about it!" the general says. Then he says to us, "Make yourselves fires! When they see us warm under the protection of our gods, they'll give up theirs by noontime!" Instead, they sit out there and freeze to death!

LUCIUS    All for want of denying their god.

VITO    Well, a couple have come in.

LUCIUS    Only a couple. *[He watches intently.]*

VITO    And now they're nice and warm. I'm not. I'll develop a death of a cold. I wish they'd give up. Or hurry up and die.

LUCIUS    Why do they do it? *[Vito shrugs.]*

VITO    You wouldn't find me freezing in the middle of a lake for our gracious god Caesar. But I think I've said that.

LUCIUS    Why don't they just march in here, deny their god, and then go home and worship him anyway? What difference would it make?

VITO    Do you know we hung this god they're dying for? *[Lucius looks at him.]* Oh, yes! I helped do it. Nailed him up on a cross as a criminal!

LUCIUS    They worship a man?

VITO    A man named Jesus. He said he was the Hebrew God, or the Son of the Hebrew God. Something like that. The heads of the Jewish sect couldn't stand it, said it was blasphemy. I don't know why. Our Caesar says *he's* a god. Every time we turn around the Senate is declaring someone, somewhere, a god.

LUCIUS    What did he do to inspire this kind of worship?

VITO    Nothing spectacular. He healed sick people, and that was amazing to watch. I saw it once. A boy full of devils. He fed thousands of people with a handful of fish, I heard.

LUCIUS    And that wasn't spectacular?

VITO    *[Shrugging]* For all the excitement it did nothing to free Israel from Rome, did it? He spent most of his time talking with poor people, with outcasts. He made himself a particular stench to the holy men.

LUCIUS   Can you imagine? A god who spends his time with the outcasts instead of the generals and the kings!

VITO   It's crazy. But it's no matter. He went too far and the holy men decided to put him away. We were only too happy to comply. The Jews can be trouble, and doing nothing with this Jesus might have caused a riot. So we crucified him.

LUCIUS   They're sitting out there on the lake, freezing to death, for a dead man.

VITO   *They* say he rose up from the dead.

LUCIUS   Did he?

VITO   *[Shrugs]* Who knows? The tomb was empty. Witnesses said they saw him for several weeks. But the story from the guards was that they fell asleep and someone stole the body. I never saw him, anyway.

LUCIUS   Does he live? What do you think?

VITO   Have you ever seen a dead man rise?

LUCIUS   *[Turning his attention again to the people]* Have you ever seen people so dedicated as to die for their belief in a god—unless they knew he was alive?

VITO   Well, if their God is alive, he should use lightning to destroy this entire legion and set his "ice men" and women free, don't you think? *[Amazed]* All they have to do is come in here, say "Caesar is my god, not Jesus," go home, and worship as they please. What kind of men are they!

LUCIUS   True men. They are sons of God.

VITO   You'd best watch your tongue. General Janus would not like to hear that.

*Lucius stands and begins to remove his armor and sword.*

VITO   What are you doing!

LUCIUS   I must find out more about this God they die for.

VITO   If you go out there, it's over! Janus will declare you've joined with them!

LUCIUS   Why do you think I'm leaving my armor? I don't plan to come back.

*He exits down the aisle. Vito watches, amazed. He gets up, removes his helmet and lets it fall to the ground. He removes his cloak, then feels the bite of the cold. He puts the cloak back on and fits the helmet to his head, as he watches the people on the ice.*

VITO   What kind of people would do a thing like that? Idiots.

*Not entirely convinced by his own words, he sits and warms his hands at the fire.*

*END*

# 25

# SECOND HABAKKUK

"Then I heard the voice of the Lord saying, 'Whom shall I send? And who will go for us?' And I said, 'Here am I. Send me!'" (Isa. 6:8).

Jesus gave us our most important, and most difficult, assignment in Matthew 28:18–20: "Go into all the world and spread the gospel!"

That might mean just telling our friends, family, and neighbors. But God may have set you aside for a bigger task as well—uprooting yourself and going to another country, living in primitive conditions and strange societies, all for the love of total strangers.

It's a frightening task, and one we shouldn't take on too lightly. Nor is it one we should dismiss lightly. Obedience to Jesus can be difficult, but it is richly rewarding, especially when we remember that we will be rewarded in heaven for the things we give up here.

Surrender your selfish desires and promise to do whatever God asks. He won't give you an assignment you can't handle or in which you can't find happiness. Take courage, as Jeremiah did when the Lord promised to make him like a fortified city against his enemies (Jer. 1).

* * *

*Characters:*
HABAKKUK
TRINITY

*This is a poetic play. Habakkuk may be male or female.*

*The story:*

*The prophet Habakkuk in his day questioned God about the evil and God's apparent silence. Habakkuk offered his complaints, and God responded with answers. The book, then, was written in a poetic dialogue format. And so, in a more modern rendition, this is "Second Habakkuk."*

*Staging:*
*The set is simply a chair, its back to the audience. Habakkuk sits on the chair, arms folded across its back so that he/she faces the audience. During the course of the skit, Habakkuk will walk about. Trinity is offstage.*

*Alternative Staging:*
*The set is simply two chairs, their backs to the audience, each with their upstage side turned in (toward center). The characters begin by sitting on these chairs, arms folded on the backs so that they are facing the audience. While they speak to each other, Habakkuk does not address the other actor directly, but speaks as though addressing God in heaven. He/She moves about the stage as the scene progresses. Trinity remains seated throughout, and does speak directly to Habakkuk. Do not play Trinity like some booming, resonating, impersonal thing, but as friendly, loving, and fatherly.*

## SCENE ONE

HABAKKUK   Come on. *Prioritize.* What are you doing with your world, Lord Father? Why aren't you speaking out?

TRINITY   And why aren't you, my child?

HABAKKUK   *[As though the answer is obvious]*
  I can't. I mean, what can we do?
  I'm only one.
  *She's* only one.
  *He's* only one. . . .

TRINITY   How many ones add up
  to meet the pain,
  to seek the sick,
  to love and witness to the lost,
  to end the crime and shelve the hate?

## SCENE TWO

HABAKKUK   I love you, Father.

TRINITY   *Do you love me? And are you my child?*

HABAKKUK   How can I do it?

TRINITY   Close your eyes. *[Habakkuk does.]*
  Look up. What do you see?

HABAKKUK   A man upon a cross.
  Torn and shredded flesh flashing
    scarlet ribbons on pale skin,
  thorns designing trails of blood.
  The trembling of his fingertips,
  Nails in his wrists and feet.

TRINITY   Fingertips that touched a blind man—

HABAKKUK   Blind as me?

TRINITY   —and taught some frightened
    fishermen to love so much
  a world was changed.
  All that love died on a tree
  so it could whisper to the world through
    such . . .

HABAKKUK   . . . As . . . me.

## SCENE THREE

HABAKKUK   You know I love!

TRINITY   *[Chuckling]* Oh, yes. Yes, you love:
  Cars, computers.

HABAKKUK   Dogs and cats,
  ten-speed bikes and floppy hats,
  popcorn, movies, ice-cream things,
  George and Abe in fed mint green,
  Paychecks, Mediprin, morals taught.
  Well, nowadays, that's morals bought.
  Taxes coming! What's the use?
  Feathered pillows, minus goose,
  Cages built for zapping bugs,
  Teddy bears with sewn-on hugs,
  London Broil to warm my gut
  and extra-sausage Pizza Hut!
  My veggies grow from underground.
  I don't know if I'm up or down
  or in or out with all this stuff,
  and still I do not have enough!

And *you* . . .

want me . . .

to love the poor?

I cannot do that anymore.

The sick? The cruel? The rich? The lost?

*Pause.*

TRINITY   Do you remember Pentecost?

## SCENE FOUR

HABAKKUK   Income, family, leisure time.
  There's other things I . . . *need* . . . to do.

TRINITY   A man died on a cross, for you.
  His blood ran hot, not lukewarm,
  when it covered him:
  his brow . . .
  then nose . . .
  then lips . . .
  then chin . . .
  it ran along his chest and then
  it stained his hips, his thighs and knees,
  it traced his shins, dripped from his feet:
  every muscle cried in pain and love for you.

HABAKKUK   That was then!
  He *had* no place to lay his head.
  I have a bed.
  I have so much
  I can't give up . . .
  God? It isn't fair.
  I'm grateful, Lord.
  The poor, oppressed?
  I'll pray for them.

TRINITY   Do you know that they pray for you?
  They've everything. You've nothing, friend.
  Look upon that cross again.
  His flesh: like bloody pennants torn.
  That man, he made a universe
  and then surrendered it for you.
  Can you do as much for men?

HABAKKUK   I can't.

It hurts too much.

I *should.*

I *will.*

*[Softly:]* How can i do it?

TRINITY   That's how. Change big "I" to little "i."

HABAKKUK   *I don't know how to do it!*

TRINITY   Then *prioritize.* Lift up trusting eyes.

HABAKKUK   *[On knees, hands clasped in prayer]*
  Make my love feel pain, Sweet Jesus. I love
  them. Don't forget . . .

TRINITY   Then you *do* love me.

HABAKKUK   *[Spreading arms]* Hold me, Jesus?

TRINITY   You *are* my child.

HABAKKUK   *[Bringing his arms together, as if he
  is held in an embrace]* Prioritize.

*END*

# 26

# THE SAVAGE

## A ONE-ACT PLAY IN THREE SCENES

"Then I remembered what the Lord had said, 'John baptized with water, but you will be baptized with the Holy Spirit.' [So when they believed in the Lord Jesus Christ,] who was I to think that I could oppose God!" (Acts 11:16–17).

Prejudice—when *anyone* hates others simply because they are different.

There is also a kind of Christian prejudice when one looks down on another person and doubts his salvation because he is different—physically, culturally, socially, or in the finer points of his beliefs.

The savage in this play isn't necessarily the Indian. The most godly man becomes a savage when he begins to make his own rules regarding who qualifies for God's grace. In this one-act play, Emmers cannot accept that God would actually extend grace to someone so primitive and different as Shogut, his Indian guide.

Christian prejudice can be finer than that, however. One man will claim another isn't Christian because he buys a Sunday paper or has a particular diet, or if he doesn't attend church as often as the first Christian thinks he should.

"Accept him whose faith is weak, without passing judgment on disputable matters," Paul told the Romans (14:1). What he meant was, there are certain things explicitly stated in the Bible regarding salvation, and we can determine someone's Christianity by those criteria. Have they repented of their sins? Do they accept Jesus Christ as personal Savior? Other matters, however, aren't directly addressed (music, diet, and so forth). While we can discuss the merit of such things, Paul warns us not to pass judgment.

Patience, love, and sometimes tolerance are the best ways to deal with Christians who do things we simply do not understand!

\* \* \*

*Characters:*
  EMMERS, a minister on his way
    to Alaska
  ADDOCK, his burly guide
  SHOGUT, Addock's friend, an
    Indian guide
  THREE NOOTKA WARRIORS

*For list of props, see index, page 167.*

### SCENE ONE

*The time is the late 1800s. The place, the western Canadian wilderness. On stage are one or two logs and a fire (most likely a few sticks set as an imaginary fire). To one side is a backpack. Trees, dark*

141

*and foreboding, may be painted on flats and set upstage.*

*Emmers stands to one side, fidgeting with the pack. He glances occasionally, with contempt, at Shogut, who sits near him, wrapped in a blanket. Addock tends the fire and the potatoes which cook in it. There is also a coffeepot on the fire, and each character has a tin cup from which to drink the brew.*

ADDOCK   Hey! You gonna take all day gettin' that jerky, Preach? You're starvin' a good man t' death!

EMMERS   *[Flustered]* A moment, Brother Addock, please! A moment!

ADDOCK   *[Mumbling to the fire]* You kin hardly tell these 'taters from the coals now.

*Emmers ignores the grumbling as best he can. He finally comes up with a package of jerky and pulls from it some ugly slabs of meat. Shogut looks at him curiously, then grins and holds out his hand.*

EMMERS   *[Coldly]* Well?

*Shogut says nothing, and after a moment turns from Emmers' indignant glare.*

ADDOCK   Well, Preach?

*Emmers sighs and goes to him, giving him half the jerky.*

ADDOCK   It's about time! *[He pulls a potato from the fire, juggles it to cool it, yipping and whistling the whole time, then pops it, whole, into his mouth.]*

EMMERS   *[Indignant]* Brother Addock!

ADDOCK   *[Chewing vigorously]* Hmmmmm?

EMMERS   The Lord left his command to bless the bread!

ADDOCK   This here's a p'tater.

EMMERS   *And* the potatoes.

*He bows his head, waits a moment, then clears his throat irritably. Addock catches the hint and bows his head.*

EMMERS   Lord, we thank thee for thy loving guidance and thy care. We thank thee for thy great providence in delivering us, thy servants, thus far to thy unled flock in Fairbanks, where I shall deliver thy wonderful Word. We are thankful for thine infinite mercy upon us, unworthy though we must certainly be for such a divine and wondrous gift! We thank thee for thy Son, who shed his blood on a cross on Mount Calvary for all men, for as it is said in thy Book of Books, in the blessed Gospel of St. John . . .

ADDOCK   *[Exasperated]* This ain't a Sundy sermon, y'know.

EMMERS   *[After a cold pause]* And we thank thee, O Lord our God, our blessed Redeemer, for the bread. In Jesus his Son's holy name . . . who died on the cross for us all . . . Amen.

ADDOCK   *[Laughing and waving a potato in Emmer's face]* You fergot the p'taters, Preach! *[As he greedily begins his meal:]* I've knowed men in pollyticks, couldn't hold their wind like you an' one o' your short blessings. I bet you hit Sundy loaded for b'ar.

EMMERS   All I do, I do to hold grace with the God Almighty.

ADDOCK   You pray to old Almighty very much?

EMMERS   Six times daily.

ADDOCK   He must have almighty powerful ears.

EMMERS   "And whatsoever ye do, do it heartily, as to the Lord."

*He sits and Addock hands him a cup of coffee.*

ADDOCK   Hey, Preach.

EMMERS   Yes?

ADDOCK   I'm yer brother, huh?

EMMERS   Of course. All men are brethren in God.

*Addock considers this a moment, then slurps noisily at his coffee. He flips a thumb at Shogut.*

ADDOCK   So why ain't he your brother? Why ain't Shogut?

EMMERS   *[As Shogut looks up]* Why, whatever do you mean?

ADDOCK   I mean that, he's my friend. He's a man! And you won't even let him sleep in camp.

EMMERS   He's a savage, Brother Addock! It would be unsafe for us to keep him here after we've turned in.

ADDOCK   He's a thing o' God, ain't he, Preach?

EMMERS   A bear is a thing of God. Do we take bears into our confidence? Listen: a bear hunts, it tracks. Why, it even has its own special grunts and snarls to convey meaning. But is that grumbling bear our brother?

ADDOCK   *[Yelling]* Now looky here! Shogut ain't no b'ar!

EMMERS   *[Emphatically]* But he *is* a pagan! He follows no Christian laws. He does not know . . . *cannot* know our ways! *[He pauses a moment to calm himself, then with a smile tries to console Addock.]* Can't you see? He worships the stars and the fish and the dead.

ADDOCK   *[Still shouting]* But he's bin Christianized!

*This comment throws Emmers into a frantic rage. He slams down his cup and paces about, gesticulating, as he preaches.*

EMMERS   Christianized! You cannot "Christianize" his kind! You can expose him to the true love of God, yes! And tell him of our sweet Lord Jesus' life and death and rising from the grave, yes! But his mind has been closed by Satan. Look at him! He can barely understand me when I speak in the merest monosyllables.

ADDOCK   I don't hear you talkin' so good in his tongue.

EMMERS   Because *his* tongue is not the tongue of God! His mind, his soul's hope for salvation, all lie locked beneath the dark shades of his savagery! A "man" who was raised praying to dead men's souls cannot comprehend our God. He's the stock of Cain!

ADDOCK   That's a lie!

EMMERS   Do you think this pleases me? No! I would that he was wise like us, unto the ways of our benevolent Lord. He is a slave of talismans and chants, and cannot change by any power short of God's own interventions . . . and God has leased his kind to Satan. I don't know why. I know only that it is good, because it is of God. Enough: perhaps we are safe with this savage in daylight, but I'll not trust to have him sleeping near me in the night.

ADDOCK    Now . . . !

EMMERS    There are other things to be done! Feed the sled dogs and set him to his duties. You're paid too well to spend the hours arguing the ways of God with a theologian.

ADDOCK    And where will you be?

EMMERS    Saying my devotions and prayers. In those trees, I think. [He removes from the pack an immense Bible and seems to fairly stagger under its weight.] I'll say a word for you, Brother Addock.

Addock stares in disbelief, but suddenly the preacher's whole attitude seems tremendously funny to him. He laughs.

ADDOCK    Throw one in for the savage, Preach.

Emmers looks at him coldly and Addock's smile fades, turning into an equally cold glare. Emmers exits and Addock watches until he is gone, then turns to Shogut, who is rolling out bedrolls.

ADDOCK    Let me give you a hand, there, buddy.

## SCENE TWO

Morning. Emmers is asleep in his bedroll while Addock's bedroll lies empty. Emmers awakes to see Shogut on the log, chewing Emmers' boot. Astounded, Emmers struggles out of his roll, jerks the boots from the surprised Indian and raises a hand to strike him.

EMMERS    My boots!

ADDOCK    [Running in with a gun] What's goin' on!

EMMERS    Your noble savage is eating my boots!

ADDOCK    [As Shogut shakes his head in denial] He's just tryin' to make friends, Preach!

EMMERS    By eating my boots?

ADDOCK    He's softenin' 'em up fer yer feet! It's a sign o' humility, shows he likes you, God knows why. He wants to bury the hatchet.

EMMERS    In my back, no doubt.

ADDOCK    It'd even up for that cross you stuck in his. Shogut, you go git that smoked bacon down from the tree. We was savin' it for later, but we'll eat it today, seein's how we won't be able to later, maybe. [Shogut leaves.]

EMMERS    Why not?

ADDOCK    [Absently] Huh?

EMMERS    I said, why won't we?

ADDOCK    [Casually] Cause we got troubles.

EMMERS    [An echo] Troubles.

ADDOCK    [In affirmation] Troubles.

EMMERS    [Thoughtfully] Troubles . . . ?

ADDOCK    [Absently] Uh-huh.

EMMERS    Troubles?

ADDOCK    [Shouting] Troubles!!!

EMMERS    What kind of troubles?

144

ADDOCK    We lost two of our best dogs in the night.

EMMERS    Dear Father in heaven! Wolves?

ADDOCK    More 'n likely Indians.

EMMERS    Indians?

ADDOCK    [Impatiently] Noble savages!

EMMERS    Are you sure?

ADDOCK    Wolves ain't known for leavin' arrows in their prey.

*Shogut enters with bacon wrapped in a bundle, which he sets on the ground.*

SHOGUT    Bacon.

ADDOCK    Ah! Siddown, gentlemen, siddown! Shogut, tell Preach Emmers here: we got Indians on our tail?

SHOGUT    Three days now.

ADDOCK    That's it! Dazzle 'im with yer golden tongue! Tell 'im who and how many.

SHOGUT    Four. Five. Noot-ka braves.

ADDOCK    Talks like Will Shakespeare. A reg'ar immortal beard.

EMMERS    He said Nooka?

ADDOCK    *Noot*ka. They're usually out on the coast. They make them totem poles.

EMMERS    And he's known for three days? Why didn't he tell me?

ADDOCK    [Grinning] Ask an' ye shall receive, Preach.

EMMERS    Are they after our supplies?

ADDOCK    More 'n likely after *us*. Band o' God's anointed white folks slaughtered a tribe of 'em not long back, I unnerstand. Wiped out the whole camp: women, kids . . . took their furs an' fish. I think they call that 'manifoot destiny' or somethin' down in the states. I reckon they're both hungry and mad, Preach. Like a big ol grunting b'ar. [He pauses to pour himself coffee, and slurps noisily.] Guess they jus' don' unnerstan' the ways of a lovin' God.

EMMERS    We've got to get out of here!

ADDOCK    With our two best dogs gone, we're grounded. Can't outrun 'em, an' only got one gun. Me or Shogut, we might make it on our own. Be tough, but I guess we could do it. But don't worry about yourself, none. We ain't gonna leave you. After all, you got God on your side, right? [He gives Emmers a playful wink and begins to unwrap the package.] Let's eat, Preach.

EMMERS    [Taking some comfort in Addock's ease] Shall we . . . bow our heads, then? [They sit: Emmers, then Addock, then Shogut.]

ADDOCK    Yeah. But this time, Shogut gives thanks.

EMMERS    Him? A heathen? Blasphemous!

*Although Addock's response comes in a noisy shout, there is some of his infectious cheeriness in it, and he grins broadly. On the last word, he is nearly in Emmers' face, his jowls rattling as he shouts.*

ADDOCK    I said, HIM! A HEATHEN! BLAS-*PHEEEE*-MOUS!

145

*He now sits on the other side of Shogut, intentionally putting the Indian between them. Shogut watches him, confused.*

ADDOCK   Go ahead. That one they taught you in the missionary place.

SHOGUT   God . . . Thank you for . . . good meat.

God . . . thank you . . . bread . . . we eat.

*He smiles suddenly and puts his arms around Emmers and Addock's shoulders. Addock smiles as well, but Emmers stares in surprise and disbelief.*

SHOGUT   God . . . thank you . . . for good friends.

God . . . keep us safe. A-men.

### SCENE THREE

*Emmers is alone in the clearing, with his Bible. He is obviously nervous, afraid, and trying to find comfort in the Word. He flips to a passage and begins to read:*

EMMERS   "Plead my cause, O Lord, with them that strive with me. Take hold of shield and buckler, and stand up for mine hope. Draw out the spear, and stop the way against them that persecute me. Say unto my soul, I am thy salvation. . . . "

*As Emmers reads, a warrior sneaks up on him from off stage, carrying a knife in his right hand and a rifle in his left. Shogut enters from opposite the warrior and yells:*

SHOGUT   PREACH!

*He charges, knife in hand.*

EMMERS   [*Who does not see the warrior*] Dear God in heaven!

*The following with, perhaps, the help of a strobe light: Shogut runs past Emmers and grabs the warrior. The two struggle across the stage. Meanwhile, Emmers has dropped his Bible and quickly picked up the rifle which the warrior has dropped. Shogut raises his knife and kills the warrior, who falls. Warrior 2 now rushes down an aisle, screaming and carrying a spear. He and Shogut circle one another, and Shogut is stabbed. Painfully, he looks at the horrified Emmers and the gun he carries, then collapses and dies. Emmers shoots the warrior.*

*Lighting returns to normal. Emmers looks at the man he has just killed and wipes his own face in a near-panic. He now crosses, stumbling, to Shogut. The Indian lies facing the audience, his eyes open in death and one hand raised slightly, as if waiting for something to be put in it.*

EMMERS   Well, what are you waiting for, my friend? Jerky? A . . . prayer? If any of your kind could reach salvation, it would be you, Shogut. You've shown something much like love beneath that savage heart. This is an irony: Brother Addock was out searching for savages, and instead they found us. This is providence.

*Emmers rises, takes up his Bible in one hand and the rifle in his other. Feeling confident now that the danger is past, yet still a little dazed, he begins to exit. Just as he passes the flat, however, warrior 3 jumps out, screaming a terrible war cry. Emmers screams at the same time, in terror. The warrior embraces him tightly as rifle falls. The embrace is lethal: his back is broken and he falls dead. The warrior stands over his victim. His face is painted red and black, and he screams like some demon over his victim. There is a shot offstage, and the warrior runs.*

*Addock enters, carrying his gun. He hesitates over whether to pursue the warrior and decides not to. He crosses to Shogut and cradles his head, closing his dead friend's eyes, then seizes the hand with his.*

ADDOCK   Don't pay no mind, Shogut, I'll see
ya in glory. I know I will!

*He remains there a moment, mourning his friend,
then folds the dead man's hands across his chest. He
crosses to Emmers, whose eyes are also open in death.
Emmers clings to the Bible, which Addock tries to
pull loose, but can't. He stands, looking up at the
sky.*

ADDOCK.   I give yuh yer saints, Lord.

*He takes the second gun and exits.*

*END*

# APPENDIX

## Directing Holy Thespians

# DIRECTING HOLY THESPIANS

## A MORE OR LESS BRIEF PRIMER ON DIRECTING THEATER

*If you are totally inexperienced with directing, this primer will be great help. If you are fairly (or greatly) experienced, you might browse through it as a quick refresher course. Its aim is to aid the novice director in running an effective, efficient rehearsal and performance.*

### DEALING WITH YOUR ACTORS

#### Parent-Child, Director-Actor

Alfred Hitchcock once said all actors should be treated like cattle. But I prefer to think the director-actor relationship is of the parent-child mentality. I don't say this because you are directing youth—the same is true if you're directing your peers, your elders, professional actors or novices who couldn't tell the difference between a stage direction and a Pittsburgh street map.

As the "parent" you must be firm and apply discipline. Let everyone know, right from the start, that . . . "We're here to have fun, but we're here to work as well. Please respect the people who are on stage by being quiet, so they can concentrate on what they're doing. If you feel you must talk, go to another room, but always be sure I know where you are so I can get you when I need you."

Be friendly, but firm. As your "children" they have certain rights, too. Set a rehearsal length and stick to it—don't detain them just because "every-

thing is going so well" (or so badly). *Do* let them know, however, that if they tie up forty-five minutes' time by socializing, you will feel free to hold them an additional forty-five minutes. And STICK TO IT. You'll be amazed how obedient everyone is next time.

And if you don't stick to it? Look in the dictionary under "chaos" for a description of any future rehearsals.

#### Problem Children

There are a few typical problems you'll run across regarding actors. Number One, I think, is convincing them to speak loudly enough to be heard two feet away. Remind them how important it is to be loud—and that, when the sanctuary is full, the actors' voices are going to be swallowed up that much more—human bodies are great sound absorbers. Fire this cardinal Director's Rule #1 at them:

IF YOU FEEL LIKE YOU'RE SHOUTING, YOU'RE ALMOST LOUD ENOUGH.

Other common problems:

The biggest ham will suddenly freeze up on stage (conversely, at times, your best-pressed wallflower comes alive when he's got a part to hide behind). People sometimes won't use their imaginations on stage, fearing they'll overdo it and look stupid. Employ Director's Rule #2.

HAM IT UP—IF YOU OVERDO IT, I'LL LET YOU KNOW.

Of course there are the hams who want to be the star at every moment—and they'll steal scenes the best way they can. Try to convince them that over-acting can be as big a crime as under-acting. The guy who stands out because he hams it up so much looks as much a total fool as the guy who comes out and draws a total blank on his lines.

Another problem is actors who can't work together.

WHEN THERE'S NO TEAM SPIRIT, THERE'S NO SHOW.

And that is Director's Rule #3. What causes this? Many things—one pushy, ham actor can do the damage. So can personality conflicts. If Connie and Charles have just broken up, it wouldn't be wise to have them acting with one another. You might have shy actors, or kids who simply don't like other kids—youth aren't generally good at hiding their negative feelings toward other youth. But take heart—drama is one of the best ways to teach teamwork and team spirit. How do you overcome this problem? Lectures, talking to actors privately, wisdom in casting, prayer—basically, playing Solomon.

Finally, you get the actors who enunciate as though they've got mouthfuls of yogurt. Solution? Drill them. Try some tongue twisters. Replace words in the script which they cannot pronounce with ones they can.

To address problems of actors—especially when there is a lack of cooperation or personality conflicts—set the actors down and talk to them about the problem. Don't identify problem actors by name (and I include, "I won't mention any names, but her initials are . . . "), as that will isolate them and very likely worsen the situation. Tell the actors where the problems lie. Encourage them. Tell them not to be afraid to act. They'll look better if they do and sillier if they don't. Tell 'em to yell—if they get too loud you'll let them know. Give 'em a real *rah-rah-sis-boom-bah* speech.

And when this fails (and it certainly will), try a few theater games.

## THEATER GAMES

The games listed are useful in correcting many of the problems common with actors, and are also good as general ice breakers. Each game is number-coded as to the problems it addresses. Code:

1. Imagination/emotion.
2. Relating to actors/items on stage (play these games if the actors seem wooden or awkward on stage).
3. Teamwork, breaking the ice.
4. Voice (Volume and diction problems).

### Team Charades: 1, 2, 3

Write scenes or situations (some suggestions are below) on slips of paper and put them in a bowl. Divide your actors into two or three teams and have a captain draw a slip from the bowl. The teams take turns acting out their scenes without words while the other teams guess what is being portrayed. For an option: let them talk.

Give each team a couple of minutes to discuss how they'll present their scene. They must all be involved in the scene and portray it actively. For instance, if they are to portray a hamburger, they can't simply have someone sit and pretend to prepare a hamburger and eat it. They must be the hamburger. One person can build the burger with parts made up of the other actors. One is a bun, another the patty, the others are the condiments. If bowling, one person can be the bowler, another the ball, and another the tenpins.

SUGGESTIONS:

*Sports.* Football, soccer, bowling, tennis, pool, hurdles, hockey, roller derby, professional wrestling, Frisbee.

*Meetings.* Church service, board meeting, revival, school, the principal's office, firemen at a fire, choir practice, a picnic.

*Jobs.* Reporter, secretary, pickpocket, thief, policeman, politician at a rally, dentist, bag lady, preacher witnessing to hoods, Mr. America, incompetent electrician.

*Abstracts.* Bacon and eggs, cheeseburger, brushing teeth, old jalopy, bear trap, reclining chair, washing machine and dryer, television set.

## Hunter and Hunted: 2

Imagine that you're in a small arena, and that the arena is littered with obstacles. It is pitch black. On the other end is someone you must avoid but who must, at all costs, capture you. When the bell sounds you have three minutes to avoid him.

That's the idea behind this blindman's buff style game. It is especially good for teaching actors to better relate to objects on stage, as the players must carefully touch and feel their way around the many obstacles and booby traps. Immensely popular with youth, you may find them demanding to spend a whole night playing.

First, get two volunteers to be Hunter and Hunted. They should be taken to a separate room where they are blindfolded by their guides. Now, mark out your arena: a fairly large room will work, or you might mark off the corners with chairs and rope. Clutter the entire area with chairs, step ladders, small tables, books, trash cans and piles of light objects that, when toppled, will make noise. Be careful not to use any item that a blindfolded person could get hurt on.

Disorient the contestants by spinning them, then place the Hunter in one corner and the Hunted in another, facing each other. On your signal they have three minutes: the Hunter seeking the Hunted, the Hunted avoiding the Hunter. Make sure one doesn't simply lay on the floor and wait the three minutes out. That destroys the whole purpose of the exercise. Each must rely on his or her sense of hearing and touch the whole time.

Be certain the actors not participating remain quiet.

After the three minutes are up, have at least one more round so that everyone will be able to watch. Afterward, discuss how the players related to the items in the arena, touching and handling each thing with which they came in contact, and how they related to one another.

## Machine: 1, 3

More of an exercise than a game, this one is quick and easy.

Explain that you're going to construct a machine, and that each person is going to be a part of that machine. One person will start the process by making himself the machine's core.

To do this he will stand, making a machine-like noise, and adopting a machine-like motion (he may spin, pop up and down, pump his hands or head back and forth, whatever). Now, one at a time, the rest of the actors will become part of the machine. They may act as a wheel or gear, convey things from one part of the machine to another part, or whatever they wish, so long as their action directly ties to the action of the machine part preceding them. The trick is to remain in motion at all times and make sounds.

The end result is a noisy, fun machine that accomplishes absolutely nothing other than to break the ice, teach teamwork and encourage imagination.

## Alphabet Conversations: 1, 4

This little improv uses two or three actors while everyone else watches. Use a scene suggested below or invent your own. The actors must act out the incident. They can talk all they want but they can only use constant repetition of the alphabet as their language (A B? C D! E F G.) Their expressions and actions must be what gets the point across.

SUGGESTIONS:

At the restaurant with a bratty child.

A phone call between angry lovers.

A husband and wife battle over control of the television.

A TV salesman hawking his Romco Everything Dicer.

## One Fine Day: 1, 3

Without explaining why, ask three people to whisper something in your ear. They can say absolutely anything that comes to mind: a saying, a dumb comment, a question. Write their words on three pieces of paper.

Now get someone to call out a place: a beach, airport, hospital, etc.

Finally, ask for three kinds of people one might find in such a place: a doctor, nurse, poet, minister, lawyer, old man, nerd, whatever.

Enlist three volunteers. Assign one of the above mentioned characters to each, and hand them one of the written phrases. Don't let them reveal the phrase to anyone. Explain that they must act out the scene together, using any dialogue or action that comes to mind but that they must find a way to use the assigned phrase and have it make sense.

Some of the phrases you'll get will be a real challenge, especially after the first round. I once found myself as a passenger in a luggage pick-up section of an airport, having to ask, Have you seen my dead octopus?

## Bible Improvs: 1, 3

Divide the actors into teams. They must present a story or parable from the Bible, which may be assigned or chosen by lot. The actors must perform the story without words while the others try to guess what the story is. An alternative: they act out their stories while one person reads it from the Bible.

## Moods: 1, 2, 4

After everyone has learned their parts, select a scene and run it as it is supposed to be run. Then run it again with these variations:

- Everyone mad at each other.
- Everyone depressed.
- Everyone excited.
- A mixture of the above.

Some scenes can really be comical when acted this way.

## Tongue Twisters: 4

A strict diction and volume game, this one can be played two ways:

1. Select two teams and line them up, opposing teammates facing one another. Select a tongue twister and read it. Now each team must repeat your selection, one player saying the first word, the second player the second word and so forth, working up the line and down again. They have to say it a total of three times, without mistakes. Time them. Repeat with the second team. Whoever says their tongue twister fastest wins.

2. Form a circle. Go to one person and slowly repeat a tongue twister. He must then repeat it to you, quickly. If he slips up, he is out of the game. If he repeats it quickly, he then goes to another person and gives them a tongue twister. If he cannot say it right himself, he is out of the game. This same process goes on until only one person remains. When you run out of known tongue twisters, try making them up. Here are a few I know:

Rubber baby buggy bumpers.

*Peter Piper picked a peck of pickled peppers. If Peter Piper picked a peck of pickled peppers, how many pickled peppers did Peter Piper pick?*

How much wood could a woodchuck chuck if a woodchuck could chuck wood?

*Two toads tied together tried to trip to Tripoli.*

Badly bungled, Betty Baker baked a bungled bagel badly.

*If you are a rat or a bat, Ararat is where it's at.*

She sells seashells down by the seashore.

*The sixth sick sheikh's sixth sheep's sick.*

Donna Dagle devours date danish on her dates with dirty Dana.

*See the slow ship sinking slowly in the salty sea?*

## THOUGH I SPEAK IN THE TONGUES OF MEN AND DIRECTORS . . .

Like any craft or career, actors have their own language. They cross. They steal. They cover and turn out. They go above and below, into the wings and sometimes even into the flies.

You don't need to know the whole bank of terminology to direct skits, but knowing some of the basics of blocking terminology and theory certainly helps. Let's look them over. Memorize them, and teach them to your actors!

*Blocking.* Blocking is how, when, and where your actors move about on stage. It is both a noun and a verb, the act of determining stage movement and the result, as well.

## FIGURE 1

| Up Right | Up Center | Up Left |
|---|---|---|
| Right Center | Center | Left Center |
| Down Right | Down Center | Down Left |

**Audience**

*Business.* This is anything the actors are doing on stage: twiddling their thumbs, examining a sculpture, slapping together a sandwich, or slapping around a flunky.

*Props.* Short for properties. Props are any items being used that can't be called part of your set or costumes. Pens, books, guns, notepads, etc., are all props.

*Up, Right, Down & Left Stage. (See Figure 1)* To avoid confusion, directions on a stage, like a compass, never change. If you stand in Pennsylvania and face north, north is north. If you turn and face south, however, north is still north. And east is always east, no matter which way you as a person happen to be standing.

Imagine your stage sectioned off into nine squares: three deep and three across. The three rows going from the right to the left of the stage are called Right, Center, and Left stage. They are named from the point of view of the actor looking out over the audience. Be careful to remember this: it means that, as the director looking at the stage from the audience, Right Stage is always to your left, and Left Stage always to your right.

The three bands running from front to back are Down Stage, Center Stage, and Up Stage. Down is toward the audience. Up is away from the audience. Knowing the history of these terms helps in remembering them: in the 1600s, when stage terms were being developed, the stage itself was raked, that is, built at a slant. The part closest to the audience was lower than the back of the stage. Hence, Down Stage was literally down; Up Stage was literally up.

When you overlay these two grids, you get your nine directional squares referred to as Up Right, Up Center, Up Left, Right Center, Center, Left Center, Down Right, Down Center, and Down Left. Some directors further divide the stage into Far Left and Right, resulting in fifteen possible directions. I've never known anyone to further divide into Way Down and Way Up, which would result in both twenty-five possible directions and nearly certain insurrection.

*Plains.* If you imagine your stage comprised of invisible lines parallel to the front of the stage, these are plains. If actors are standing on the same plain, they are of equal distance from the front of the stage.

*Levels.* Levels are just that—different heights from (and including) the stage floor. You place actors on different levels when you stand one on a platform and keep another on the floor.

*Actors' Positions.* (*See Figure 2.*) This fine, upstanding actress is demonstrating *positions*, which is the simplest way to tell an actor which way you want his or her body positioned in relation to the audience.

*Crossing.* If you want to tell your actor to cross the stage, you aren't suggesting he whip out chalk and draw religious icons. Rather, you are telling him to move. If you want him to move from a chair located at Up Left Stage to a stool at Down Right, you simply tell him to cross from the chair to the stool. If you want him to move from that chair to the Down Right area, but to not sit, simply tell him to cross Down Right.

## FIGURE 2

Full-Front

One-Quarter

Profile

Three-Quarters

Full-Back

## FIGURE 3

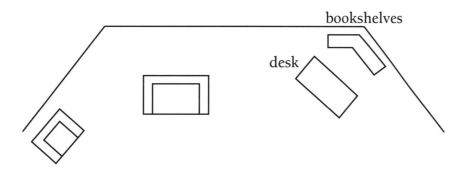

*Above & Below.* Crossing refers to movement. Above or below is how you cross in relation to an object or another actor. The easiest way to explain is by example:

An old couch sets in the center of your stage. An actress sits on it. You have an actor at left center and you want him to cross to right center. To get there he has to go around that flea-eaten couch and the young lady on it. You can tell him to go *above* the couch (that is, upstage of it, between the couch and the back wall) or *below* the couch (in other words, down stage of it, between couch and audience). If the actor who is crossing is speaking or is doing something particularly important, you will want him to cross below. If the actress on the couch is speaking or involved in important business, you'll want the actor to cross above her.

*Turning In & Turning Out.* Very simple: if you want your actor to turn (or face) toward center stage, tell him to turn in. If you want him to turn (or face) away from center stage, tell him to turn out.

## STAGE MOVEMENT ILLUSTRATED

### Log Book

It is wise to put together a prompt book. While a director's log for a full-length play can be extensive, keeping a log for a collection of skits should be pretty simple: keep a sheet of paper in the book listing the names and phone numbers of your actors and other people helping in the production, along with another sheet listing rehearsal times. Also, be sure to write all your blocking—*in pencil*—in the margins of your script.

Insist that your writers do the same, using pencils because you may desire to change the blocking at some point. You needn't write blocking in full sentences. Use the following shorthand:

First, draw a quick, freehand sketch of your stage, using squares, rectangles, circles, and other symbols to represent chairs, desks, etc. (See Figure 3.)

These are your symbols for actors. Initial them by the character's name (or the first two letters of the name, should more than one character start with the same letter).

## FIGURE 4

An arrow means to cross. The circle at the arrow's tail represents the actor's position before he moves. The circle at the arrowhead shows

## FIGURE 5

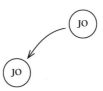

## FIGURE 6

where the actor ends up as a result of the cross. Make things easy on yourself—sketch only the part of the stage you need to get the point across, or block a number of movements into one drawing as explained below.

You may also use the following written shorthand: "X" means cross. Stage areas are identified by initials: UR for Up Right, CS for Center Stage, DL for Down Left, etc. A "2" means "to," and so on. (See Figure 6.) The sentence in this illustration reads, "John crosses up right stage to Jennifer." You might also number the lines on the text of each page, and refer to those line numbers in your stage directions:

## FIGURE 7

Your directions will be clearest (for yourself, at least) if you use the diagram and sentence forms together:

Figure 8 refers to the following action: At line 15, Tom and Alice enter through a door located Up Center. Tom crosses to a bookshelf at Up Left. At the same time Alice crosses to the couch, going around its Right Stage side, and sits. Later, on line 20, Tom crosses below the desk (located in front of the bookshelf) to the left of the couch, where he talks with Alice. Five lines later he crosses below the couch (as indicated by the arrow) and sits on the chair, located Down Stage Right.

### Crowd Control

A crowd scene can be a frightening thing for a director. How do you place them all on the stage in such a manner that they can all be seen, and so that it doesn't look like chaos? (See Figure 9, page 160.) How does the audience know which actor to watch?

The answer lies in the old maxim of divide and conquer: split your big crowd into groups, like Leonardo daVinci did in the *Last Supper*. Groups of three or four work nicely, lending order to the stage and complementing the character on whom the audience should be focused. (See Figure 10, page 161.)

You can draw attention to that primary character of the moment by having him or her move while the others are immobile, or vice-versa. You might also have the others looking at him or her.

## FIGURE 8

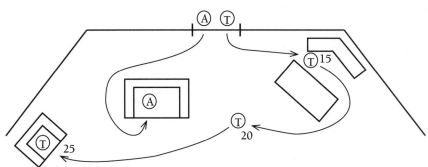

ℓ 15: Ⓣ x 2 bkshelf as
ℓ Ⓐ x US and R of couch; sits.
ℓ 20: Ⓐ looks up as Ⓣ x 2 couch, sl. side.
ℓ 25: Ⓣ x 2 chair, sits.

## PLAYING MIND GAMES

There is something very psychological about theater. You *want* your audience to feel a particular way about a story, the actors, and so on. Don't rely entirely on the ability of the actor; you'll have a decided edge if you use these little "mind games" which manipulate the audience's subconscious and helps control how the audience perceives characters and situations.

### Strength and Weakness

By that we mean psychological strength or weakness of a character as a whole, or of his situation at a particular moment.

It isn't always bad to have a character being in a weak position; rather, it adds some contrast and flair. The strong character is simply the one who—at the moment—has the upper hand, or is the one most noticed by the audience. The weak character might be humble (a shepherd in the presence of a king) or in a particularly tight spot (Jesus before Pilate).

Here are ways to portray character strength through blocking:

Put her on a higher level, such as standing on a platform or a chair.

Have her stand while everyone else sits.

Have several characters surround her in a semicircle, while she is at center stage.

Place her either full-front or profile.

Place her in a strong stage area. These areas are, in order: Down Center, Down Right, Down Left, Center.

If a person crosses from left to right stage, she is strong. If she crosses from right to left, she is weak. This is because a person, trained to read from left to right, will also view the stage from his left (stage right) to his right (stage left). If someone is walking in the same direction to which his eyes naturally follow, their movement is less noticeable and weaker. If someone crosses in opposition to the "left to right" eye flow, he is more noticeable and, therefore, stronger. In cultures which read from right to left, the opposite becomes true.

Some weak positions:

Anyone in an upstage area, unless the upstage person is talking to a person who is downstage. This forces the downstage person to turn his back—making *him* the weaker.

Anyone with his back to the audience, or standing three-quarters. One-quarter is not generally weak, unless it is next to someone standing full front.

Anyone sitting or kneeling—especially when others are standing—is usually weak.

A lone person is weaker than a crowd, but stronger than any single individual within the crowd.

### Isolation, Alienation, and Anger

The best way to let the audience know a character feels isolated emotionally is to isolate him physically. Put him in a place where no one else is, probably down left or down right. Then group the other actors together somewhere else. Or have him face one direction while everyone else faces another direction.

For anger, keep your angry characters apart from who (or what) they're angry with. The farther apart they are, the madder they seem—especially if they're having a conversation at the same time. This same idea works for getting across the idea of alienation; the farther apart the characters are, the more alienated they are.

If you want anger portrayed as a strong confrontation, put the two together, facing one anoth-

# FIGURE 9

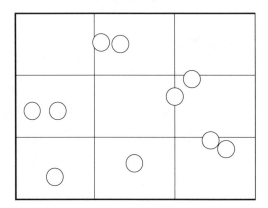

**Figure 9**: In this scene, Miss Nelson is trying to organize a ball game. Somehow the kids don't seem to be listening. Even if they were all facing her, the over-all effect would be chaotic.

# FIGURE 10

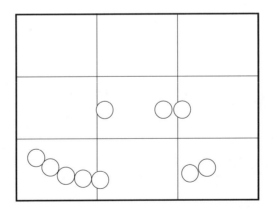

**Figure 10:** Here, however, everyone pays attention. It is easy for the audience to follow as well.

er. If both are standing in one-quarter positions, you've got a decent debate. If they're standing profile, you're close to a brawl. Such characters are in *very* strong positions. The first actor who leaves this profile position will give the idea of being the weaker of the two.

## Personal Space

Persons who get along well use a lot of eye contact and feel comfortable while being physically close. The closer you place them, the friendlier they seem.

Casual acquaintances and strangers never sit very close unless forced to. They don't want to invade anyone's personal space, nor have theirs invaded.

For these reasons you can get two effects by having people sit right next to each other: with lovers, you have intimacy. With strangers, you have instant tension—as long as those moods are helped by decent acting.

Likewise, placing lovers far apart on a bench suggests conflict—the trust seems gone. But put two strangers far apart on a bench and they'll strike up a friendly conversation.

## Body Language

The Sea Witch in Disney's *The Little Mermaid* was right. "Don't forget the importance of body language." The more "open" your body is, the more relaxed and trustworthy the audience thinks you are. The more drawn in or "closed" you are, the more tense or deceptive you appear. Thus, if a character is feeling guilty or is up to no good, you might have him fold his arms, cross his legs, or hug himself.

## Breaking the Rules

Like the rules of everything but salvation, the only unbreakable rule is that there's no unbreakable rule. You'll find situations where these rules and suggestions don't quite apply, or when you can actually get a better effect by violating them. But as a general rule they are, as Paul would say, "true and trustworthy."

## SETS, COSTUMES, AND PROPS

Most of the plays in this book and most skits in general require no special effects and most often call for simplified sets and basic props. Here are some suggestions to help you along, however.

For starters, secure the help of a seamstress and a carpenter for your plays. In churches this is generally easy to do. There are several people handy with wiring, hammers, and sewing machines who are ready to help.

## Flats

When the skit calls for a wall, a forest, castle, or trees in the background, a flat is the easiest way to represent such background scenery. To make a flat, simply build a 4'x8' frame out of furring strips or 1x3 lumber, using screws inserted in triangular plywood plates at the corners to hold it together. Make as many as you need.

Next get enough unshrunk muslin to cover the framework. Using a staple gun, attach the muslin, stapling it to the edges. This should be a two-person job: the muslin needs to be stretched as tightly as it can so that it is like a drum.

Mix a solution of six or seven parts water to one part of white glue. Paint this liberally over the muslin and let it dry. Then paint it with a coat of white, acrylic-based paint.

Once this is dry you can paint any scene on it you wish. Flat, as opposed to glossy colors, are best. Once the skit is over, you can paint another layer of white paint over your flat and repaint a new scene on it. Thus, your initial investment of time is well worth the effort, since flats are easily stored, repaired and reusable.

If the flat is ever ripped, simply take a bit of muslin, soak it in white glue and water, and stick it to the back side of the flat as a patch.

## Other Backdrops and Set Pieces

Use your imagination. I have seen the cardboard rolls used by carpet layers turned into beautiful palm trees, and many other ingenious devices. Many newspapers will let you take the end rolls from their press runs, giving you a plentiful supply of newsprint in large dimensions, which can be used for large banners or papier maché.

A number of recipes are available for papier maché as well; consult any art teacher or home economist.

When constructing objects out of papier maché, use buckets, balloons, or framework covered with chicken wire for your skeletons. Often you can paint backdrops on cloth and staple that to platforms or walls to complete your set.

## Costumes

For funny costumes (granny costumes, loud and clashing costumes, and cheap, tacky jewelry), just launch an invasion on a secondhand store, and seek the donations of church members who aren't too embarrassed to admit they ever wore such things.

Biblical costumes are easy to make—they are simple vests, one-piece tunics or even sheets simply wrapped and pinned around the actor. Invest in some cloth to make a ready reservoir of these items. If your children's Sunday school papers don't offer ready pictures of the costumes you need, go to a college library where books on costumes through the ages can be found.

## Makeup

Sometimes you'll want to use a little makeup—to show a guy looking pretty dirty; to portray an old person (wrinkles around the eyes), or an animal.

For this reason, be sure you collect any wigs you can snag; again, the secondhand store is a good source.

Also, about Halloween time, stock up on tubes and cups of makeup (available at most department stores). This is quality stuff, and washes off with soap and water.

## Oddities

Do you need a sword? Armor? Some odd kind of hat or gun? When your home church and the department stores can't produce what you need and you can't dream up a way to make it on your own, there are alternatives.

Many large communities have costume rental shops and theatrical supply stores. Check your Yellow Pages and contact your local high school or college to find out where their drama program gets supplies.

If there are no such stores available, there's always mail order. A number of theatrical supply companies provide anything from mustaches, wigs, crowns, and jewelry to makeup, stage lights, fog machines and curtains. They're usually quick to send supplies, and always happy to mail a catalog.

Two of the better:

Norcostco Costumes
3203 N. Highway 100
Minneapolis, MN 55422–9975
(612) 533-2791

Rubies Theatrical
One Rubie Plaza
Richmond Hill, NY 11418
(718) 846-1008

## CONCLUSION

And there you have it. Remember, when doing anything for the Lord we are responsible to do our best. Put the information in this appendix to work, and you'll be amazed at how well your skits will go. Your youth can look as polished as any grown-ups. Don't underestimate the importance of your role as director, or in the ability of your young actors.

Break a leg!

# ALPHABETICAL INDEX OF PLAYS

## Key to Abbreviations:

+ or - means one or more characters could be added or deleted with minor changes in the script.

M/W means the part(s) could be played by either men or women.

*means the part could be played by a woman, although this might require minor script changes (primarily names).

### Advice and Adonijah

*Characters:* 1 M/W. *Set:* A chair, down center. *Costume:* Old jeans, plaid shirt, walking shoes, bandana.

### Brother's Keeper

*Characters:* 1 man. *Set:* A table and chairs. *Costume:* Modern dress. *Props:* Scene One—on the table a breadboard, a sharp knife, a loaf of unsliced bread, a jar of peanut butter. Scene Two—with Cain, a bag of groceries. The groceries: an apple, cans of Green Giant asparagus, mandarin oranges, pineapple chunks, Pepperidge Farm Soup.

### Daniel #1: The Friends Who Obeyed God

*Characters:* 6-9; 3 men, the remainder M/W. *Set:* at stage left a table and four chairs. *Costumes:* Bible period. You might make your king plump. *Props:* King—Whiffle® Bat. Ashpenaz—notepad and pen. Narrator—marker and three blank name tags.

### Daniel #2: The King's Dream

*Characters:* 6+; 3 men*, 3 or more M/W. *Set:* possibly a chair as a throne. *Costumes:* Bible period. *Props:* Daniel—marker and large pad on an easel (or an overhead projector). Arioch—"Humphrey Bogart" hat, trench coat, tommy gun or sword.

### Daniel #3: The Fiery Furnace

*Characters:* 8; 4 men*, 4M/W. *Set:* A "fiery furnace" made of a couple of refrigerator boxes taped together and painted up. *Costumes:* Biblical except as noted. Fire—yellow pants and shirt. *Props:* King—Whiffle® Bat. Chaldeans—a newspaper, cue cards.

### Daniel #4: The Dream of the Tree

*Characters:* 9+; 1 man, 1 woman, 7-10 M/W. *Set:* A bed. *Costumes:* Biblical except as noted. Tree—brown shirt and pants. Animals—costumes suggesting characters. Pruner—safari hat and coveralls. *Props:* Tree—branches, a decorative bird, a banana and apple. Pruner—clippers, written speech, a glass of water. Ashpenaz—an iron, an air horn, a glass of water. Nebuchadnezzar—feather. *Sound Effects:* Recording of *Nutcracker Suite.*

### Daniel #5: The Handwriting on the Wall

*Characters:* 9+; 2 men*, 1 woman, 6-9 M/W. *Set:* a long table and several chairs at one side of stage, a wall panel—possibly made of cardboard—on the other. The wall should have a section cut out, with paper glued over the hole. This is what the hand will burst through to do its writing. *Costumes:* Biblical. *Props:* Hand—Felt marker. Daniel—Pointer. Belshazzar—Golden cup, Whiffle® Bat. Soldier—Whiffle® Bat.

### Daniel #6: The Lions' Den

*Characters:* 7; 2 men*, 5M/W. *Set:* A lions' den (the reverse side of that fiery furnace) with a stepladder beside it. *Costumes:* Biblical except as noted. Darius wears a silly golf outfit and crown. Lions have "lion paw" gloves. *Props:* King Darius—golf club, two golf balls, an empty glass. Guard—a Whiffle® Bat. Ashpenaz—notepad. Satraps—magnifying glasses.

### Education Interview, The

*Characters:* 3; 1 man, 1 woman, 1 M/W. *Set:* 3 chairs at center stage in an interview format. *Costumes:* Modern. *Props:* Pusher—several reports and folders.

### Fable of the New Age Pig, The

*Characters:* 8 (+ or -). 1 man, 1 woman, the rest M/W. *Set:* Center stage, a fence with an axe leaning against it, and a chair or stool in front of the fence. Down left, a small table with two chairs. *Costumes:* Pigs—pig noses. Farmer—bib jeans and a cap. Farmer's Wife—"country" dress with apron. Dog—Dog nose. *Props:* Farmer—Axe, pail, plate of pork bones. Wife—Coffeepot. Table—Two coffee cups.

### Ice Men

*Characters:* 2 men. *Set:* Two stools or benches. Optional: a "fire." *Costumes:* Roman soldiers. *Props:* Swords, blankets, helmets for each soldier. Note: actors may also use pantomime to "illustrate" their costumes, thereby doing their roles in modern dress.

### Judgment Jeopardy

*Characters:* 6-7; 3 men*, 1 woman, 2-3 M/W. *Set:* Jeopardy board if possible, comprised of nine panels with categories of three questions each (answers printed on revolving panels as shown in script). Three podiums at left stage, with contestants' names hand-scrawled across the fronts. If you can rig it, lights at each podium (to identify the player going for each category) really work nicely. *Costumes:* Mr. Gabe—white suit. Guards—black sweats. George—incredibly raggy-looking. Fred and Alice—modern. *Props:* Offstage—sound effects buzzer (one of those that motorists buy to zap other drivers). Mr. Gabe—microphone. Guards—kazoos.

### Manna Helper

*Characters:* 7; 1 man, 1 woman, 5 M/W. *Set:* A stool down left. Down center, a table. *Costumes:* Announcer—modern. Everyone else, biblical. *Props:* Announcer—guitar. Mother—big pot of manna.

### Matter of Worth, A

*Characters:* 3 men*. *Set:* A chair down center, a sign reading "ELISHA ESQ., MAN OF GOD" down right. *Costumes:* Biblical. Naaman as a warrior. *Props:* Elisha—a scroll. Gehazi—a broom, two lumps of gold, a "leprous hand" glove hidden in his robe. Naaman—leprous hand glove.

### Not Just Black and White

*Characters:* 6-13; 5 men*, 4 women, 4 M/W. *Set:* Up center, a desk. Over it, a portrait of Hitler or a Nazi flag. Stage right: a bench. Stage left: a table set with dinner for four. *Costumes:* 1940s, except for Alice and Jill, who wear modern dress. Constable and Officer—SS Uniform. Jew—handcuffs, patch with Star of David. Baker—apron and baker's hat. *Props:* Baker—bread. Officer—book. Mayor—pen and "proclamation." Alice and Jill—cans of Coca-Cola®.

### Procedure, The

*Characters:* 3; 2 men, 1 woman. *Set:* Upstage center, a chair. To its right, a small table. *Costumes:* Doctor—smock. Woman—modern, loose-fitting clothes. Old Man—Baggy pants and jacket, an afghan about his shoulders. *Props:* Doctor—clipboard.

## Puppet Master, The

*Characters:* 6+; 3-6 men, 2 women, 1 M/W. *Set:* row of chairs. *Costumes:* Biblical. Judas in green. If you stage the Puppet Master, you might put him/her in black tights. *Props:* Puppet Master—marionette sticks.

## Quicker Moral-Upper, The

*Characters:* 3 women. *Set:* A table. On it, a cup which will be knocked over. *Costumes:* Modern. Rosie wears an apron. *Props:* Alice—a vase with goldenrod. Rosie—a cup of liquid, two copies of "The Daily Devotional," made up of a double-folded sheet of paper with its title written across. The inner pages are made of folded-up tissue.

## Real Stew, A

*Characters:* 4; 3 men, 1 woman *or* 2 men and 2 women. *Set:* Bare, except for a stool down left. *Costumes:* Biblical, except Dan/Murky who is modern dress. *Props:* Dan/Murky—microphone. Esau—bowl and spoon, also a dead animal (stuffed toy—skunk works best).

## Restaurant Christians

*Characters:* 2 M/W. *Set:* A table, as in a restaurant. *Costumes:* Modern. *Props:* Two menus and water glasses.

## Reunion, The

*Characters:* 2 men*. *Set:* A park bench or three chairs set together as a bench. *Costumes:* Modern. *Props:* Kirk—large book.

## Savage, The

*Characters:* 6; 3 men (speaking); 3 men* (non-speaking). *Set:* Upstage center, a backdrop of barren trees. Down center, a camp fire surrounded by two or three logs. Scattered about: bedrolls, a large backpack, one rifle. Cooking utensils around the fire. *Costumes:* Emmers and Addock—late 1800s. Emmers in conservative clothes and long coat; Addock a backwoods mountain man. Shogut and Warriors—Indian costumes. *Props:* Scene One, Addock—potatoes, tin coffeepot, 3 tin cups. Emmers—beef jerky, large Bible. Scene Two, Shogut—Emmers' boots and a package of bacon. Scene Three, Emmers—large Bible. Shogut—knife (preferably collapsible). Addock—rifle; Warriors—#1, collapsible knife and rifle; #2, collapsible knife. Nonspeaking Indians in war make-up with #3 most terrifying.

## Second Habakkuk

*Characters:* 2; 1 man, 1 M/W. *Set:* A chair. *Costumes:* Modern.

## Spiritually Fed

*Characters:* 5; 3 men, 2 women. *Set:* three chairs, stage right; at left stage a desk with one chair behind it and another chair at its right stage side. *Costumes:* Modern. A "grandma" wig for Mrs. Roberts. *Props:* Desk—notepad, books, small calendar, family picture, metal letter opener, knick-knack. Mrs. Roberts—a bag of knitting items and a six-foot-long sock in progress.

## Well-Pegged

*Characters:* 4; 2 men, 2 women, 1 M/W. *Set:* Scene One: a palm tree (or backdrop) and a stool, center stage. Scene Two: the same stool at center; upstage right a tent. *Costumes:* Narrator—modern. All others—biblical. Sisera's should be tattered and torn. Jael's should be loose and flowing, and she should have lots of bangles and jewelry. *Props:* Jael—a wooden mallet, tent peg, and a "bull's eye" target on a paper clip.

## What's the Answer?

*Characters:* 6-8 M/W. *Set:* Center stage, four chairs. *Costumes:* Modern except for Crusader and Moslem, who should be medieval. *Props:* Crusader and Moslem—swords. Optional: Hoods—crowbars. Youths—newspaper.